1

Book 1: DevOps Handbook

Introduction to DevOps and its impact on Business Ecosystem

BONUS DEVOPS BOOKLET

Dear Friend,

I am privileged to have you onboard. You have shown faith in me and I would like to reciprocate it by offering the maximum value with an amazing gift. I have been researching on the topic and have an excellent "DevOps Booklet" for you to take your own expedition on DevOps to next level.

- Do you want to know the job requirement of DevOps Engineer?
- Do you want to know statistics of DevOps job available and mean salary offered?
- What are the latest trends in DevOps methodology
- People to follow on the latest on DevOps development

Also, do you want once in a while updates on interesting implementation of latest Technology; especially those impacting lives of common people?

"Get Instant Access to Free Booklet and Future Updates"

- Link: http://eepurl.com/dge23r

- QR Code : You can download a QR code reader app on your mobile and open the link by scnning below:

Contents

Introduction

DevOps is the buzzword these days in both software and business circles. Why? Because it has revolutionized the way modern businesses do business and, in the process, achieved milestones that weren't possible before. And in this book, you'll learn what DevOps is, how it evolved, how your business can benefit from implementing it, and success stories of some of the world's biggest and most popular companies that have embraced DevOps as part of their business. It is my hope that by the time you're done reading this book, you'll have a good idea of how DevOps can help your business grow.

So if you're ready, turn the page and let's begin.

Chapter 1: What is DevOps

DevOps – or development and operations – is a term used in enterprise software development that refers to a kind of agile relationship between information technologies (IT) operations and development. The primary objective of DevOps is to optimize this relationship through fostering better collaboration and communication between development and IT operations. In particular, it seeks to integrate and activate important modifications into an enterprise's production processes as well as to strictly monitor problems and issues as they occur so these can be addressed as soon as possible without having to disrupt other aspects of the enterprise's operations. By doing so, DevOps can help enterprises register faster turnaround times, increase frequency of deployment of crucial new software or programs, achieve faster average recovery times, increase success rate for newly released programs, and minimize the lead time needed in between modifications or fixes to programs.

DevOps is crucial for the success of any enterprise because, by nature, enterprises need to segregate business units as individually operating entities for a more efficient system of operations. However, part of such segregation is the tendency to tightly control and guard access to information, processes and management. And this can be a challenge, particularly for the IT operations unit that needs access to key information from all business units in order to provide the best IT service possible for the whole enterprise. Simply put, part of the challenge in segregating business units into individually operating ones that are independent of each other is the relatively slow flow of information to and from such units because of bureaucracy.

Moving towards an organizational culture based on DevOps – one where the enterprise's operations units and IT developers are considered as "partners" instead of unrelated units – is an effective way to break down the barriers between them. This is because an enterprise whose culture is based on DevOps is one that can help IT personnel provide organization with the best possible software with the least risk for glitches, hitches, or problems. Therefore, a DevOps-based organizational culture is one that can foster an environment where segregated business units can remain independent but, at the same time, work very well with others in order to optimize the organization's efficiency and productivity.

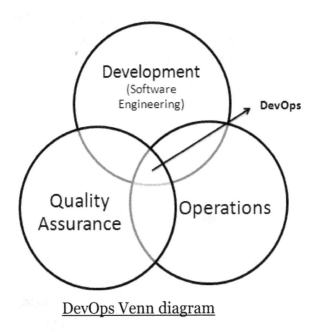

DevOps Venn diagram

Key Principles

One characteristic of DevOps is that it isn't grounded or dependent on stringent processes and methodologies. It's based more on key principles that allow an enterprise's key business units to efficiently work together and, in the process by breaking down any "walls" that may prevent optimal working relationships among such units. These key principles that guide an enterprise's DevOps are culture, measurement, automation and sharing.

Challenges Solved By DevOps

Just before the development of DevOps, it took several teams to collate the necessary data and informational requirements as well as writing code. After that, another team – a QA team – performed tests on new codes in a separate software development environment once the necessary requirements were met. Eventually, it's the same QA team that releases the new code for deployment by the enterprise's operations group. After that, the deployment teams are divided further into groups referred to as "silos" which include database and networking. And if you consider all the teams involved with the development and deployment of just one code, you won't be surprised why many enterprises suffer from project bottlenecks.

With such a set up, several undesirable things happen. One is that developers often become unaware of roadblocks for Operations and Quality Assurance that may keep the new programs from working as they were designed to work. Another thing that may happen is that as the QA and Operations teams work on so many features of the program, they may not have a true understanding of the purpose and value of the programs that are being developed/tested, which may keep such teams from effectively doing their work on such programs. Lastly, inefficiency and unnecessary backlogs are highly probable given each team or group has their own goals and objectives to achieve, which often times oppose those of the other groups, as well as the tendency to absolve themselves of responsibility for things that go wrong.

With DevOps, these potential problems can be addressed via creation of cross-functional teams that collaborate and share a common responsibility for maintaining the systems that are responsible for running software and other programs, as well as for prepping up the software so that they run on said systems with excellent feedback mechanisms for possible automation issues.

A Typical Scenario That Illustrates the Need for DevOps

Imagine that an enterprise's development team (the Dev team) releases a new program "over the wall" to Quality Assurance – the QA team. At this point, the QA team assumes the responsibility of discovering as many errors as possible in the new program, if any. Without any good working relationship – or any relationship at all for that matter – chances are high that the Dev team will be very defensive about the errors found by the QA team on their newly developed program, especially if there are lots of them. At which point, it's highly possible for the Dev team to even blame the QA team for such errors or bugs in the program. Of course, the QA team will deny that it's them or their testing environment that's to blame for the errors or bugs and that at the end of the day they're just there to discover bugs that exist within the programs developers create. In other words, the QA team will just revert the blame for the errors back to the Dev team. It can become nasty.

Let's say, after several attempts, the bugs and errors were fixed and the program has fully satisfied the QA team. They now release the program to the operations team concerned, a.k.a., the Ops team. But the Ops team refuses to fully implement the new program

14

because they feel that too much change too soon will hamper their ability to do their jobs effectively. So they limit their system's changes. As a result, their operating system crashes and blames the Dev team for it, notwithstanding the fact that their refusal to implement the system fully led to the crash.

Defending their honor and glory, the Dev team blames the Ops team for not using the program the way it is designed to be used. The blaming continues on for a while until finally, someone has the sense to intervene and eventually lead the teams to cooperate their way into fixing the program. But the delay and the losses were already incurred.

The Continuum

One very practical way to look at the various DevOps aspects is to use what's called the **DevOps continuum**. The vertical axis represents the 3 delivery chain levels of DevOps, which are continuous integration (lowest level), continuous delivery, and continuous deployment (highest level). The bottom horizontal plane or axis represents people's perceptions of what DevOps is focused on, where the left side represents an automation or tools perspective while the right side represents a culture perspective. Others feel strongly that DevOps must be focused more on culture than tools while for others, it's the other way around.

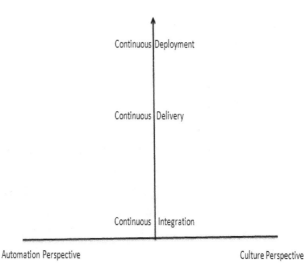

Continuous Deployment

Continuous Delivery

Continuous Integration

Automation Perspective   Culture Perspective

DevOps Continuum

The ideal location is the upper right hand corner, i.e., continuous deployment under a cultural perspective. Organizations that are located at this part of the continuum are considered as endangered species or unicorns simply because they're few and far in between. **Very good examples of these "unicorns" include Etsy,**

Netflix, Flicker, Amazon, Google and Pinterest.

Bloggers, coaches and some thought leaders usually paint a DevOps picture that's located on the upper right corner of the continuum. They may also have a strong bias towards either tools or culture. While it's not necessarily bad to have robust debates or discussions as to which is more important (tools or culture), the fact remains that organizations need both in order to optimize their productivity. Culture won't be productive without the necessary tools and tools won't work properly without the support of a very good culture.

It's important for organization to realize that moving up to the DevOps Nirvana spot in the continuum takes time. Many times, the first move is to combine tools, culture and continuous integration, which is at the lower wrung of the continuum. It shouldn't be an issue because DevOps isn't a very simple and easy activity and as such, it takes many baby steps and some time to maximize.

An optimal DevOps may be different for each organization because it's a blend of tools, culture, and maturity, all of which should make sense. And those that make sense is often relative and can change over time. What's crucial here is are continuous efforts to minimize – or even eliminate – any obstacles or bottlenecks for each software delivery phase through improvements in the automation processes and collaboration between silos or business units.

DevOps Maturity Phases

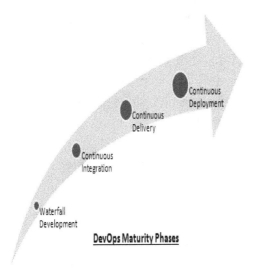

DevOps Maturity Phases

In order to keep track of an organization's DevOps progress, it's important to be cognizant of the maturity phases involved in DevOps. These include:

Waterfall Development: Prior to continuous integration, development teams write a ton of code for several

20

months. When they're done with writing code, the teams will then combine their finished codes together so that they can release it. The code will come with different iterations or versions that are so different from each other and would probably undergo quite a number of changes that its integration process may take several months to complete. As such, this process may be considered as an unproductive one.

Continuous Integration: This refers to the quick integration of newly developed code with the existing main code body that will be released. This phase can help the team save a ton of time, especially when they're ready to release the code already.

This phase or process wasn't conceptualized by DevOps. Continuous integration is a practice that originated from the Extreme Programming methodology, which is an integral part of an engineering process called Agile.

While it's been around for quite a while, this process or term was adopted by DevOps because every successful execution of continuous integration requires automation. As you learned in the DevOps continuum, continuous integration is the first level of the DevOps maturity phase. This involves checking codes in, collecting it into a binary executable code in most cases, and doing basic testing to validate the code.

Continuous Delivery: This phase may be considered as an extension of the previous one and is stage 2 of the DevOps stage. During execution of this DevOps phase, adding extra automation and testing is needed in order to make newly developed codes ready for immediate deployment with practically no human intervention whatsoever. This is a good way to augment an organization's need to be able to frequently merge newly developed codes with main code lines. At this phase, an organization's code base is in a constant state of ready deployment.

Continuous Deployment: This shouldn't be confused with the previous phase, continuous delivery. This is considered to be the most advanced DevOps phase and is a condition wherein organizations are able to deploy programs or codes directly to production without the need for any kind of human assistance. As such, it's considered to be the "nirvana" of DevOps and this makes companies "unicorns."

Teams that make use of continuous delivery never deploy codes that aren't tested. Instead, they run new codes through a series of automated testing procedures prior to pushing them to the production line. Typically, only a small percentage of users get to receive newly released codes where an automated feedback system is used to monitor

23

usage and quality of the code prior to full release.

As mentioned earlier, only a few companies are already in this phase – the **nirvana phase** – of DevOps because doing so takes time and serious resources. But given that most organizations find continuous integration quite a lofty goal, many often aim for continuous delivery instead.

The Focus of DevOps

Establishing a culture of collaboration and using automation (with DevOps tools) as a means to improve an organization's efficiency are the main focus of DevOps. While there's a tendency to be biased towards either tools or culture, the truth is it takes some combination of both tools and culture for an organization to become optimally productive.

Culture

When talking about culture within the context of DevOps, the point of focus is on increasing collaboration, reducing isolation of units (silos), sharing the responsibilities, increasing each team's autonomy, increasing quality, putting a premium on feedback and raising the level of automation. Most of what DevOps values are the same as those of the Agile system because it's an extension of the latter. We'll talk more about Agile later on but in a nutshell, Agile may be considered as a holistic software delivery system that measures progress through working software. Under Agile, developers, product owners, UX people, and testers all work as a tight-knit unit to achieve a common goal.

As an extension of the Agile system, DevOps involves adding an operations' mindset – and possibly a team member with some

operational responsibilities – to the team. In the past, the progress of DevOps was measured in terms of working software. These days, it's measured in terms of working software that's already in the hands of the end users or customers. This is achieved only through shared system (runs the software) maintenance responsibilities, close collaboration via breaking down of silos or obstacles to such collaboration and preparation of the software so that it'll run in the system with high delivery automation and quality feedback.

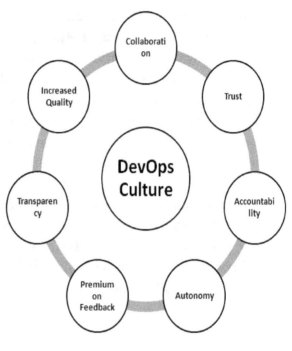

DevOps Culture

Tools

When talking about DevOps tools, we talk about configuration management, building and testing of systems, deployment of applications, control over different versions of the program or code, and tools for monitoring quality

27

and progress. Each of the maturity phases of DevOps – continuous integration, delivery, and deployment – all need a different set of tools. While it's true that there are tools commonly used in all the phases, the number and kinds of tools needed increase as an organization moves up through the chain of delivery.

And speaking of tools, some of the most important ones include:

Source Code Repository: This refers to a place where codes are checked in and changed by developers. The repository manages the different iterations of code that are checked in it, making it possible for developers to avoid working on each other's works. Some of the most popular tools used as code repository include **TFS, Bitbucket, Cloudforce, Subversion and Grit.**

Build Server: This refers to an automation tool that collects code in the source code repository into an executable code base. Some of the most popular tools include **Artifactory, SonarQube, and Jenkins.**

Configuration Management: This defines how an environment or a server is configured. Popular tools include **Chef and Puppet**.

Virtual Infrastructure: This type of infrastructure lets organizations create new machines using configuration management tools like **Chef and Puppet**. These infrastructures are provided by cloud-vending companies that sell platform as a service (PaaS) or infrastructure and include Microsoft's Azure and Amazon Web Services. Organizations can also get "private clouds", which are private virtual infrastructures that allow fur running a cloud on top of the hardware in an organization's data center. An example of this is **vCloud by VMware.**

When combined with automation tools, virtual infrastructures can help empower organizations that use DevOps to configure their servers with no need for human intervention. An organization can test brand new codes simply by sending them to their cloud infrastructure, creating the necessary environment, and running all necessary tests with no need for any human fingers to touch a computer's keyboards.

Test Automation: When doing DevOps testing, the focus is on automated testing to make sure that only fully deployable or working codes are deployed to production. Without an extensive automated testing strategy, it's hard – if not downright impossible – to achieve a state of continuous delivery with no human intervention where organizations can be confident about the codes they deploy into production.

Some of the most popular tools for test automation include **Water and Selenium**.

Pipeline Orchestration: Think of a pipeline as a factory assembly line. Further, think of this as the time when the development team finishes writing the code until the code is fully deployed in production.

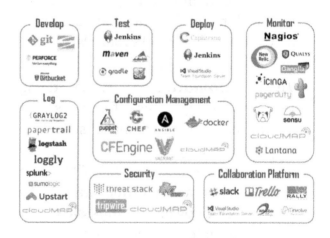

Source of above image: emaze.com

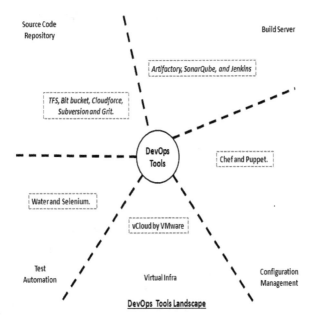

Source Code
Repository

Build Server

Artifactory, SonarQube, and Jenkins

TFS, Bit bucket, Cloudforce,
Subversion and Grit.

DevOps
Tools

Chef and Puppet.

Water and Selenium.

vCloud by VMware

Test
Automation

Virtual Infra

Configuration
Management

DevOps Tools Landscape

Chapter 2: The DevOps Evolution

Many organizations have experienced much success when it comes to using Agile methods for hastening the delivery of software. Starting from the development organization, Agile has slowly increased its scope to include other important areas like operations and information technology (IT). Teams and sub-teams have learned how to streamline processes, improve the quality of feedback mechanisms and how to speed up the innovation processes in IT departments. All of these have had significant effects on organizations' productivity.

To capitalize on these developments, continuous delivery and DevOps were created with the aim of connecting organizations' development teams with

IT operations primarily via automated systems. By doing so, organizations were able to foster an environment of increased the responsiveness, agility and faster software delivery times to the market.

Back in 2001, a document called **The Agile Manifesto** emerged from the software development environment and introduced what is now called as Agile Development. Methodologies based on the Agile system oriented software developers in the art of breaking down the software development process into much smaller bites that are called "user stories". These "stories" helped speed up feedback acquisition processes, which in turn helped organizations align their products' features with the needs of their markets much faster.

Agile focused on helping small teams and developers work much more efficiently and smarter. At first, only small software startup companies who were excited to disrupt what was then the current software market and who were willing to do that through trial and error were into the Agile system. As the process gradually evolved and matured, the whole software community started to become more and more responsive and accepting of methodologies based on the Agile system.

In turn, such increasing acceptance made the concept of "scale" more and more important in the industry. Developers were able to come out with functioning programs or software codes much faster. But when it come to the downstream processes of testing and deployment of newly developed codes, two things prevented organizations from increasing the turnaround or delivery times of quality software to their intended users: fragmented processes and the existence of functional silos, i.e., segregated operating business units.

Eventually, the Agile system gave birth to new technologies and processes that were aimed at automating and streamlining the whole cycle of software delivery. With the coming of age of continuous integration or CI, smaller and more frequent code releases became the norm as more and more codes needed to be tested and integrated daily. This in turn put a huge strain on Quality Assurance (QA) and Operations (Ops) teams.

A breakthrough book by Jez Humble titled Continuous Delivery helped promote the idea that the entire software lifecycle can be viewed as one automatable process. It was so effective in promoting said idea that even Fortune 1000 companies started embracing this idea. In turn, the perceived value of Agile initiatives that were at the time blocked and stalled and in the process, also helped increase the stakes for treating software delivery as a crucial and strategic initiative in business.

Agile focused on the needs of code developers. On the other hand, continuous delivery and DevOps initiatives helped organizations become much more efficient, productive, and profitable. These two have also helped organizations improve their software delivery cycles.

Many industry experts believe that DevOps and CD – as Agile system extensions – have the biggest chance for organizations to optimize their enterprise values. An industry expert once said about CD that if the software delivery cycle is a concert, Agile is the opening act and CD is the show's main performer.

Software-driven organizations that continue to evolve in terms of technical frameworks and processes have already transitioned from just implementing continuous integration to continuous delivery. In doing so, CD has transformed software delivery as we know it and has extended the potential of Agile by linking DevOps practices and tools with CI or continuous integration.

Continuous delivery is – from a technical viewpoint – a collection of methodologies and practices that are focused on improving software delivery processes and optimize the reliability of organizations' software releases. It makes use of automation – from continuous integration builds all the way to deployment of codes – and involves all aspects of research and development and operations organization. At the end, CD helps organizations release quality software systematically, repeatedly and more frequently to their end users or customers.

Leading software expert Martin Fowler developed key tenets for Agile-based continuous delivery, based on successful agile methodologies. He outlined key questions to ask in continuous delivery such as:

- Can the organization readily deploy your software through its entire lifecycle?
- Can the organization keep the software deployable and prioritize it even while working on its new features?
- Is it possible for anyone to receive quick and automated feedback about their applications and infrastructures' production readiness whenever a person modifies or changes them?
- Is it possible for the organization to just push a button to deploy any version of software whenever it's needed?

Extending the Agile system through continuous delivery provides organizations several benefits including:

- A faster time to deploy software to the market;

- Better quality of products;
- Higher customer satisfaction;
- Higher productivity and efficiency;
- Increased reliability for software releases; and
- The capability to create the right products.

Agile's impact in the software industry has been both highly disruptive and far-reaching. It has also helped promote new ideas outside of itself, which includes multi-functional processes (DevOps) as well as continuous delivery (CD) that impact both software end users and organizations. With the onset of DevOps and CD, waterfall approaches have been archived in the annals of software history and communication and collaboration continue to remain important aspects of an organization's operations.

Timeline

For a better understanding of the evolution of DevOps and CD, here's a timeline of crucial events in their development.

<u>*2007*</u>

A software development consultant by the name of Patrick Debois tried to learn all of IT's aspects. Within 15 years, Patrick has assumed quite a number of different roles in the Information Technology sector so that he can work in just about every role imaginable within an IT organization, the goal of which was to get a holistic yet intimate understanding of Information Technology. Developer, system administrator, network specialist, project manager, and tester – you name it and Patrick Debois has worked it.

In 2007, Patrick took on a consulting job for a huge data migration center organization and was in charge of testing. That meant he spent a huge

41

chunk of his time working with development and operations (DevOps). For the longest time, Patrick had been uneasy about how differently Devs and Ops worked. In particular, he became frustrated with the way work was managed between these two groups when it came to data migration.

That time, CI or continuous integration was starting to become very popular within the Agile circle and was brining development ever so closer to deployment. Still, there was a void when it came to bridging the huge gap between Dev and Ops. At this point, Debois had a strong sense of sureness that there has got to be a much better way for these two particular groups to work much better.

2008

Patrick chanced upon a post at the 2008 Agile Conference by Andrew Shafer, wherein the idea for a session that'll

42

discuss an agile infrastructure. After seeing the post, Patrick attended the session but unfortunately, the idea was very badly received to the point that only Patrick showed up. Not even Andrew Shafer, the brains behind the idea, bothered to show up at the session he himself called for!

But that didn't stop or discouraged Patrick Debois. With his enthusiasm over knowing he wasn't alone with his ideas or point of view concerning the divide between Dev and Ops exceeding that of a kid in a candy store, he ultimately tracked Andrew Shafer down and formed a Google group named Agile System Administration.

2009

Flickr's Senior VP for Technical Operations John Allspaw and Director For Engineering Paul Hammond presented "10 + Deploys Per Day: Dev and Ops Cooperation At Flickr" at the

43

2009 O'Reilly Velocity Conference in San Jose. This presentation provided what will ultimately become the groundwork for improving software deployment via improvements in the way Dev and Ops work together.

Though Patrick was in Belgium at the time of the presentation, he was able to catch it via live streaming. This presentation encouraged him to come up with his own conference in Ghent, Belgium: DevsOpsDays. This conference was able to gather together a very lively group of futuristic thinkers who are passionate about how to improve software development. Even more important is that the group maintained and publicized the conversation over Twitter using #DevOpsDays as its hashtag. In an attempt to optimize Twitter's limited character limit, the group eventually truncated the hashtag into #DevOps.

2010

44

In 2010, the DevOpsDays conferences were held in the United States and Australia. The conference was conducted in more countries and cities all over the world over time. And this fostered even more face-to-face meeting between like minded IT people, which in turn made more IT people excited about the idea of DevOps until it came to a point that DevOps became a full-fledged grassroots movement.

2011

Prior to 2011, the grassroots movement known as DevOps was primarily driven by open source tools and individuals with hardly any attention from software vendors and analysts. But on that year, DevOps started infiltrating the mainstream by getting the attention of top analysts such as Jay Lyman and Cameron Haight from 451 Research and Gartner, respectively. As a result, the big boys of the software industry started to take notice and even market DevOps.

DevOps – at this time – was fast becoming a buzzword in the industry. As a result, the DevOpsDays conference continued with its growth all over the world.

2013

By this time, several authors have begun writing books on DevOps as a result of the growing insatiable public thirst for information related to DevOps. Some of these authors include Mary and Tom Poppendiek with Implementing Lean Software Development, and Gene Kim, Kevin Behr and George Spafford with The Phoenix Project.

2014

Some of the world's biggest companies started to incorporate DevOps into their organization. These include Lego, Nordstrom and Target.

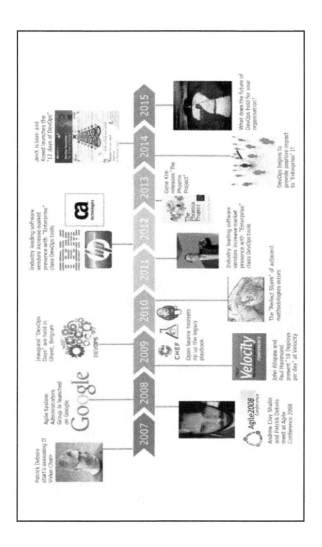

Source: Article "Evolution of DevOps" on LinkedIn

48

Chapter 3: The Agile System and DevOps/CD

From out of the need to keep up with the increasing speed at which software is developed and the increasing number of software being developed and released as a result of such increasing speed, which Agile methods have allowed organizations to achieve, came forth the DevOps. It may be considered as the love child of Agile software development, as significant advancements in methods and culture through the years have brought to fore the need for an approach to the entire software delivery cycle that's more holistic.

What Is The Agile System?

The Agile system or Agile Development is a general word used to refer to numerous incremental and iterative software development methodologies. Among these methodologies, the most popular ones **are Extreme Programming (XP), Lean Development, Scaled Agile Framework (SAF), Kanban, and Scrum.**

Despite each methodology having their own unique approach, all of them have common threads – vision and core values. All of them basically incorporate continuous feedback and iteration for successfully refining and eventually, delivering a software system. All of them also involve continuous planning, testing, integration, and other kinds of continuous evolution both in terms of the software and the projects. All of them are also lightweight compared to other old-school approaches or processes such as Waterfall-type ones. Also, these methodologies are naturally adaptable. But the most important commonality among these Agile methods is the ability to empower people to quickly and effectively collaborate and make decisions together.

At first, developers made up most Agile teams. As these teams started to become more and more efficient and effective in producing software, it became obvious that having separate development (Dev) and quality assurance (QA) teams was an inefficient way of doing things. As a result, Agile methodologies started to encompass the QA process so that the speed at which software is delivered can be much faster. Agile continues to grow, which now includes delivery and support members, so that Agile can encompass all aspects from ideation to delivery of software.

The ideals of DevOps are able to extend the development practices of Agile through the rationalization of how software moves through all stages – building, validating, deployment, and delivery. It does so while empowering cross-functional units or teams by giving them complete ownership of the software application process from design through production support.

DevOps and Agile

Essentially, DevOps is simply the expansion of principles used by Agile. It includes systems and operations and doesn't just stop dealing with concerns once codes are checked in. Aside from collaborating as a cross-functional unit made up of developers, testers, and designers that comprise an Agile team, DevOps also includes operations people in its cross-functional units. This is because instead of just focusing on coming up with a software that works, which is what Agile's all about, DevOps aims to provide customers with a complete service, i.e., a working software that's effectively and efficiently delivered to its end users or customers. DevOps emphasizes the need to minimize or even eliminate obstacles and barriers to effective collaboration between software developers and operations (end users), making the most out of their combined skills.

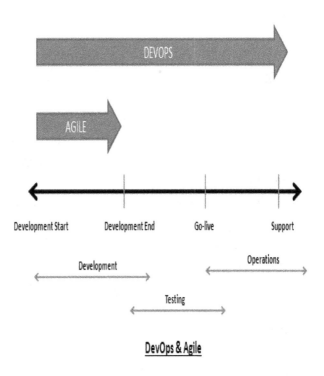

DevOps & Agile

While Agile teams make use of automated building, automation testing, continuous integration and continuous delivery, DevOps extends Agile teams a bit more to include "infrastructure as code", metrics, monitoring, configuration management and a tool chain perspective to cloud computing, virtualization, and tooling in order to speed up changes inside the world of modern infrastructure. Also, DevOps incorporates other tools like orchestration (e.g., zookeeper, mesos, and noah), configuration management (e.g., cfengine, ansible, chef, and puppet), containerization, virtualization and monitoring (e.g., docker, vagrant, OpenStack and AWS), and many others.

As you can see, DevOps is merely an extension of the Agile system that encompasses operations in its definition of cross-functional Agile teams and fosters collaboration between developers and operations in order to fully deliver working software to their end users.

Chapter 4: Scrum

Scrum refers to an Agile methodology or framework for managing projects that's primarily used for projects involving software development, the goals of which are to deliver new software features or capabilities every other week or month. Scrum is one approach that heavily influenced the document known as the Agile Manifesto that enunciates a particular set of principles and values that help guide organizations make decisions related to the faster development of high-quality software.

The use of Scrum has already encompassed other business activities such as marketing and information technology, where projects need to move along in complex and ambiguous environments. Many leadership teams also use Scrum as their Agile management method, usually mixing it with Kanban and lean practices.

Scrum and Agile

Scrum may be considered as a sub-type of the Agile software development system. Agile, if you may recall, is comprised of principles and values that describe an organization's daily activities and interactions. In and by itself, Agile is neither specific nor prescriptive.

Scrum adheres to Agile's principles and values but also includes further specifications and definitions. In particular, these additions pertain to specific practices concerning the development of software. And while Scrum was developed for Agile software development, it has become a preferred framework by which Agile projects in general are managed. Occasionally, Scrum is also called Scrum development or Scrum project management.

Some of the benefits of using Scrum include:
- Better satisfaction among stakeholders;
- Faster time to market;
- Happier members or employees;
- Higher quality products;
- Improved dynamics between teams and members; and
- Increased productivity.

This methodology can address work complexities by among other things, more transparent data or information. Through improved transparency, the organization's stakeholders can check and if necessary, adjust or adapt depending on the current or actual condition or environment the organization's in instead of projected conditions or environments. This ability to check and adjust lets organizations or teams to work on many of the common shortcomings of waterfall development processes, which include among others:

- Confusion as a result of frequently changing requirements;
- Inaccurate reporting of progress;
- Software quality compromises; and
- Underestimating of costs, resources, and time.

In Scrum software development, transparency in common standards and terms is a must so that delivered software meets expectations. Inspecting frequently helps to ensure continuous progress and help the organization detect any unwanted variations in results early enough to enable quick and timely adjustments. When it comes to inspection and adaptation, the most popular Scrum events include Sprint Planning, Stand Ups (a.k.a., daily Scrum), Sprint Retrospective and Sprint Review.

Scrum Components

The Scrum Agile development methodology is made up of key components: team roles, ceremonies (events), artifacts, and rules. Normally, scrum teams are made up of 5 to 9 members with no specific team leader who decides how to attack a specific problem or who delegates project tasks. Decision-making is a collegial process, i.e., the whole team – as a unit – gets to make decisions regarding solutions to problems and issues faced by the team. Every Scrum team member plays an essential part in coming up with solutions to problems faced by the team and is anticipated to bring a product all the way from conception to finalization.

In Scrum teams, members can take on 3 roles, namely that of a product owner, Scrum master, and the development team. A product owner is a project's primary stakeholder. Normally, a product owner is an external or internal customer, or a customer's representative. There can only be one product owner and he or she determines or communicates the project's overall mission and vision that the team is expected to build or develop. Ultimately, the product owner's accountable for taking care of product backlogs and accepting finished work increments.

The ScrumMaster role is assigned to a person who will serve as the product owner, development team, and organization's servant leader. The ScrumMaster acts more like a facilitator considering the lack of hierarchical authority over development teams, and ensures the team's adherence to Scrum rules, practices, and theories. He or she also protects the development team by doing everything he or she can to assist the team in optimizing its performance. "Everything" may include things like helping the product owner manage backlogs, facilitate meetings and remove obstacles or impediments.

The Development Team is a cross-functional unit that's self-organizing and is equipped with all the necessary skills for delivering shippable increments every time a sprint or iteration is completed. Under the Scrum methodology, the role "developer" expands to include the role of any person involved in the process of creating the content for delivery. For members of the development team, there are no titles and there's no one who tells the team how to convert backlog items into increments that can already be shipped to customers.

Ceremonies (Scrum Events)

A sprint refers to a time-boxed period in which particular types of work are finished and are prepared for review. Normally, sprints last for 2 to 4 weeks but it's not impossible to hear of sprints that conclude within 1 week only.

Sprint planning refers to team meetings that are also time-bound or boxed. These help determine which among a product's backlog items will be shipped to the end user and how to actually do it.

Daily Stand Ups refer to very short meetings not exceeding 15 minutes. In said meetings, each member of the team covers progress made in the project since the last stand up in a fast and transparent manner, any obstacles that are hindering him or her from progressing in the project and any work planned prior to the next meeting.

Sprint reviews refer to events where in the development team gets the opportunity to demonstrate or present completed work during sprints. Here, the product owner checks the work vs. pre-determined criterion for acceptance and based on such criterion, approves or rejects the finished work. Here, the clients and stakeholders also provide valuable feedback that ensures each and every increment delivered is up to the customer's needs and specifications.

Retro – a.k.a. the retrospective – refers to the final team meeting during the sprint to find out the things that went well, those that went bad, and how the development team can further improve its performance in succeeding sprints. This meeting's attended by the team members and the ScrumMaster and is a crucial opportunity for the team to set its sights on improving overall performance and determine continuous improvement strategies for its processes.

Artifacts or Documents

Scrum artifacts include product backlogs, sprint backlogs, and increments. A product backlog is possibly the most valuable Scrum document or artifact, which lists every product, project, or system requirement. The product backlog may be viewed as a list of things to do, where each item on the list is equated with a deliverable that provides business value. These items are ordered or ranked according to their business value by the product owner.

A sprint backlog refers to a list of items sourced from the product backlog. In particular, these items are those that need to be completed in a sprint or iteration.

Increments are the sum of all product backlogs that have already been addressed or completed from the time the latest software version was released. The product owner decides when to release increments but it's the team's responsibility to ensure everything that comes with an increment is ready for release. These ready-for-release items are also referred to as Potentially Shippable Increments or PSIs.

Scrum Rules

When it comes to rules that govern Scrum, they're entirely up to the team and should be determined by what is best for their particular processes. The most competent Agile coaches will instruct teams to begin with some of the most basic Scrum events discussed earlier and then review and adapt according the team's particular needs. Doing so ensures continuous improvements in how teams collaborate.

Chapter 5: Kanban

Kanban is a way of managing the product creation process. It emphasizes continuous delivery (CD) without having to overburden an organization's development (Dev) team. It's also designed to improve collaboration between an organization's different units. Kanban is based on 3 key principles:

- Visualization of the things done today, i.e., the workflow. The ability to see everything within the context of each other can provide a lot of useful information to the organization.
- Limiting the amount of work-in-progress (WIP), this helps bring balance to a flow-based approach that helps an organization's teams avoid taking on too much work all at once.
- Flow enhancement, i.e., as soon as a task is done, work is started

on the next highest order task from the backlog queue.

Consistent with DevOps and CD, Kanban helps promote ongoing collaborations and promotes active and continuous learning and improvement by defining an optimal team workflow. And for any DevOps initiative, the implicit goals are fast movement, rapid deployment, and responsiveness to a rapidly changing business environment. Kanban – as a methodology – is a very helpful and progressive tool for achieving an organization's desired outcome. In particular, the ability to be able to monitor an organization's progress and status on a daily basis instead of weekly isn't just a very appealing proposition but one that can also transform the way an organization is able to communicate and complete its tasks.

The Kanban approach or methodology helps developers work as one solid unit and finish everything they've started. If through the Kanban principle on limited Work-In-Progress a part of the development team is obligated to allocate their resources into other aspects of an ongoing project to assist in its completion, these members will be able to see the project from a larger and different perspective. This can be helpful in identifying possible issues, obstacles and bottlenecks even before they manifest and cause problems.

The ability to see projects from a holistic point of view by as much of its stakeholders as possible helps teams and the organization to adapt a system-level view. Within the underpinning principles of DevOps, this is referred to as the first way, the outcomes of which include:

- Known defects are never passed to downstream work centers;
- Local optimizations are never allowed to create global degradation;

- Continuous seeking of increased work flow;
- Continuous seeking of deeper and more profound understanding of the system; and
- Removal of the "time box" out of the equation.

Using a Kanban approach to the DevOps movement is one that requires nerves of steel because it's relatively new compared to its other Agile brothers, particularly Scrum. As such, there's much discussion about how it's more appropriate for initiatives that are time-critical like a change management endeavor or a product launch that's happening in 7 days' time. Regardless, the Kanban methodology is still one that's worth taking into consideration and checking to determine potentially beneficial changes that it may bring to an organization, specifically to its workflow. More importantly, the Kanban methodology can help an organization determine whether or not it's close to violating acceptable WIP limits. But the biggest gains that can be enjoyed from using Kanban is in finding an organization's work process constraints.

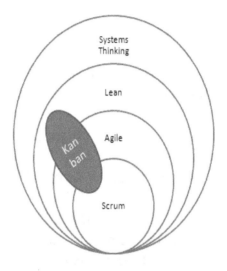

Agile Scrum & Kanban

Chapter 6: Kanban versus Scrum

With Scrum, product owners only have a limited amount of time to incorporate user stories into a sprint, which is between 2 to 3 weeks. This however poses a problem – unusual breaking points are created for people who deploy and test the software. Too little stories may not result in shippable products towards the end of iteration or sprint, may increase dependence between sprints or iterations, and may lead to very challenging coordination efforts and very difficult testing.

Using the Kanban approach on the other hand, frees up product owners from any time limitations. This is because the Kanban methodology is all about focusing on the most significant work and getting them done through processes to the right people and at the right times.

To get a better idea of the differences between the Scrum and Kanban Agile methodologies, let's take a look at two of its most crucial differences: rules and workflow.

Rules

Both the Scrum and Kanban software development methods have rules governing the performance of work. The Scrum method is the more prescriptive of the two. There are 23 mandatory and 12 optional rules for Scrum implementation per Agile Advice, which include:
- Daily meetings must be held;
- During iterations or sprints, no interruptions are allowed;
- Product owners should create and manage a backlog of its products;

- Progress should be measured using a burn-down chart;
- Teams must be cross-functional; and
- Time for work is boxed.

Collectively, such rules make for quite a rigid system in which teams must work to successfully implement Scrum in their software development. There are 2 major challenges to this. One is called ScrumBut, i.e., organizations use "Scrum, but..." This means many organizations – due to the methodology's rigidity – tend to ignore some of the methodologies rules, which leads to a non-optimal use of the Scrum framework.

The other challenge presented here is the time box, which are great for distraction-less working time for software developers to deliver specific products, and providing regular bases for stakeholders by which to steer and evaluate projects. But looking at it from

73

the lenses of DevOps, workflow is regularly broken by specific software delivery checkpoints or milestones. Such disruption in workflow makes it challenging for organizations to coordinate sprint dependencies and ensure successful transfer of software from development to production.

When you evaluate the Kanban software development methodology, you'll find that it's substantially less restrictive. Consider it only has 2 rules, which are:
- Workflow visualization; and
- Setting limits to amount of work-in-progress.

Yep – that's all folks! Having only 2 rules, this methodology is a very open and flexible one, which can be easily utilized under any environment. In some organizations, Kanban is even used outside of software development, from product manufacturing to marketing! You can even incorporate some of Scrum's work rules into Kanban if you so desire. That's how flexible it is.

Because Kanban focuses more on the workflow instead of time boxes, it's the better choice for utilizing with DevOps. Because Kanban emphasizes the optimization of the whole software delivery process instead of just the development phase, many software development experts think it's the perfect "spouse" for DevOps.

Workflow

The other major difference between Kanban and Scrum is the workflow. This particular difference is an offshoot of the difference in its rules. With Scrum, you choose the features that need to completed in the next sprint beforehand. Afterwards, the sprint or iteration is "locked," the work is performed over the sprint's duration (usually in a couple of weeks), and at the sprint's end, the cue is vacant or empty.

75

By locking the sprint in, the work team is assured of ample and necessary time for working on a problem without any interruptions from other seemingly urgent requirements. At the end of each iteration or sprint, feedback sessions help stakeholders approve or disapprove work that's already been delivered and steer the project depending on changes in the organization's activities or environment.

When using the Kanban methodology for developing software, an organization isn't subject to sprint time constraints. Instead, the much focus is given on ensuring that workflow remains uninterrupted and without any known issues as it moves downstream.

Limits, however, are placed on the amount of work queued or in progress under the Kanban methodology. It means that at any given point time in the software delivery cycle, the team can only work on a certain number of issues or features. In setting such a limit, teams are compelled to focus on only a few work items on hand, which often leads to high quality work.

A visible workflow fosters a sense of urgency for teams to keep things moving. Keep in mind that the Kanban methodology was a product of manufacturing genius and as such, its focus is on efficiency and productivity. And as it's extended to the software development arena, it incorporates important aspects of software development success like participation of stakeholders.

DevOps, Kanban, and Scrum

For organizations use DevOps, increased efficiencies, more frequent deployment of features, and high responsiveness to business demands are some of their most important goals. As such, each of the two methods can help organizations address various areas of their DevOps better than the other. While Kanban seems to be all the rage these days, it's not necessarily the automatic choice for organizations.

If an organization is responsible for developing new features that need stakeholder feedback and high developer focus, then Scrum is possibly the better choice for its DevOps. In this scenario, Scrum's sprint lock feature and demos for stakeholders at the end of each sprint or iteration can be very, very valuable to the organization.

If an organization is accountable for simple maintenance and is more reactive than the regular organization, Kanban may be the better option. This is because it has greater flexibility in terms of responding to stakeholder feedback and it doesn't require locking of backlogs.

At the end of the day, every organization's different and as such, they should know their teams' strengths and areas for improvements in order to choose the best software development method. At some point, it may even be optimal to get the best of both methodologies and combine them into one for the optimal achievement of an organization's goals.

Chapter 7 –
Organizational Culture
Change For DevOps
Success

DevOps started as a method for developing software, which was intended to hasten the software building, testing, and release processes by making two crucial teams – Operations (Ops) and Developers (Dev) – collaborate more effectively. In effect, this has to do with organizational culture.

But how exactly does organizational culture play a big role in successful employment of DevOps in organizations, particularly within tech organizations? Lucas Welch of Chef explains this by giving his working definition of DevOps, which is a professional and cultural movement that focuses on how high velocity organizations are built and operated, which is derived from its practitioner's personal experiences. He explains further that tech companies need to provide their employees a safe enough environment, enough freedom, and access to knowledge when needed if they want to succeed in a DevOps environment. Further, he explains that its team members must be empowered to think, speak, and ask without restraint or hindrance in order for them to quickly act. When done correctly, this type of collaboration among teams helps empower and engage team members with a purpose, aligned leadership, and shared sets of beliefs and values.

However, it's easier to talk about the integration of 2 teams with totally different subcultures than to actually integrate them. Based on a research done by Gartner, out of the 75% of IT departments that would've tried to come up with a bi-modal capacity by the year

2018, only less than 50% will enjoy the benefits that come along with using new software development techniques like DevOps. And according to Gartner's Research Director Ian Head, up to 90% of I&O organizations that try to use DevOps without first addressing their particular cultural foundations will eventually fail.

DevOps discussions appear to be about some new concept and methodology, but they have been circulating in the industry for long now. It's just that such concepts have gone around using different names.

But this doesn't do anything to reduce the value of the DevOps movement. Tech companies have started to get that focusing on improving collaboration between businesses units that seem to lie on opposite poles of the organization can lead to increased productivity and product quality.

Often times, the challenge in changing an organization's culture to suit DevOps are shifting the focus from the technical side of DevOps to the cultural aspect of it. It has been realized across board that organizational culture change is the most important factor for maximizing improvements from adapting this methodology.

Things to Consider

In order to successfully change an organization's culture for optimization of DevOps benefits, the following should be considered:

Dialogue Space: An organization must be able to provide a space or venue where all parties involved in DevOps can meet and talk. It shouldn't be a surprise to find that when people are asked to change the way they operate in terms of performing their functions within the organization, they'd feel anxious and resistant – at least in the beginning. An organization can help provide a very

83

good foundation for transitions like these by giving members who'll be affected by the implementation of DevOps opportunities to interface with one another in an environment that's safe and secure so that they can fully grasp the need for DevOps implementation. The organization can also ensure proper clarification of roles, responsibilities, and interdependencies to help affected members feel secure and at peace with the implementation of DevOps because often times, ignorance is the source of anxieties and insecurities.

Leader Support. An organization's leaders are some of the key stakeholders when it comes to transitioning into DevOps and as such, it must be able to provide the necessary support for them – i.e., tools, abilities, skills, and knowledge – that will enable them to lead other members through a successful transition to DevOps. Sadly, many organizations make the fatal mistake of assuming that their leaders already know what to do and have all the necessary skill sets for the job at hand. Organizations only realize such mistakes during transition, when leaders are unable to successfully lead their teams and in the process, hamper the entire transition process.

Stakeholder Engagement: In certain ways, DevOps needs key groups or teams in the organization to change their current perspectives, assumptions, and beliefs concerning how to best get their works done. By getting these groups or teams involved in the process of redefining their work along the lines of DevOps, organizations can help make them see that they are important parts of the change to be implemented instead of feeling that the organization is doing something nasty to them.

Accept Mistakes: When an organization asks their key people – most if not all of whom already have deeply-entrenched career identities – to change the way they see and think about collaborating with others to achieve a new common goal, hiccups are bound to happen despite the best laid plans and preparations to avoid them. Simply put, mistakes will happen along the way and what's more important and realistic is for an organization's leadership to react properly towards these situations because this will affect how people involved in the DevOps transition will move forward. If leaders immediately use punishment as a means of rectifying mistakes and hopefully preventing their recurrence, there's a high risk that team members will go back to their familiar place of safety – their old ways of doing things. If the organization's leaders can use mistake moments as opportunities for teaching members the proper way of doing DevOps and learn to live with such mistakes as a normal part of doing something new, the organization will be able to rebound from hiccups and glitches much faster and achieve full DevOps implementation at the soonest possible time.

Cynicism Vs. Skepticism: Skepticism in light of being presented with crucial new information about how to best get work done is normal. Consider the fact that when people have been doing their work for so many years with hardly any changes, certain key beliefs and assumptions of how to do their jobs and how to collaborate with others in the performance of their jobs become as hard as cement. So when DevOps is initially presented to them, it's ok for them to be skeptical about it. But over time, their minds will gradually change as they see the great benefits of implementing DevOps. But cynicism is an altogether different beast. While the minds of skeptics are open to the possibility of being convinced otherwise, cynics are hard set on what they think and believe to be true and as a result, they normally reject all claims contrary or not in line with their current belief systems. If skeptics believe in "guilty until proven innocent", cynics believe "immediately guilty regardless of evidences to the contrary that may be presented later on...period!" Organizations will be better off identifying the cynics in their teams and excluding them from DevOps transition and full implementation when possible.

Time: Everything worth doing successfully takes time. The only difference is how much time is needed. It's the same with organizations that are transitioning to DevOps and embedding it as part of an organization's new culture. As team members start to see more and more of DevOps benefits as time goes by, the more they'll naturally be aligned to its principles and practices. At a certain point in time, DevOps will become a natural part of an organization's culture. A fatal mistake would be to expect DevOps to be fully integrated and ingrained in an organization's culture very quickly. Doing so will lead to frustration and drastic corrective measures that can sabotage efforts instead of maximizing them.

A Holistic Approach

At the very center, DevOps is all about collaboration and teamwork. And that can only happen when people's hearts and minds are generally – not perfectly – in sync. That is the power of culture and when an organization is able to successfully foster a culture of collaboration and openness to change, then successful transition to and implementation of DevOps is not far behind.

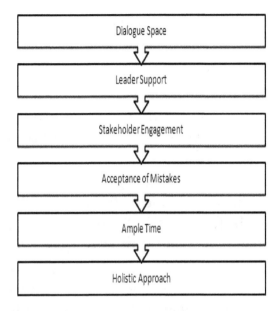

Factors for Organizational Change to adopt DevOps

Chapter 8: – DevOps Ecosystem and emerging trends

Refer the below line:

"Only 10% of companies describe themselves as fully digital." – **Datum**

Any organization, big technology firm or a small e-commerce firm, all are aiming to be fully digital. While there is a major focus on the disruptive technologies which would lead the next digital wave; the modus operandi of its execution is equally important. The true Digital Transformation can be achieved by creating DevOps culture and environment.

The DevOps Environment

DevOps is an environment, not a technology. Designing, Developing, Deploying, and Operating in a unified environment is the key aspect of DevOps methodology. Continuous deployment and integration facilitates the faster rate of software development, testing and operations. Efficiency and automation are the major pillars of this methodology.

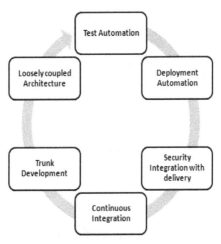

Factors creating positive DevOps Environment

To explain it further,

Automation

Automation allows the high performers of the system to focus more on innovation rather than operational activities. One example could be cited of transformation at HP LaserJet. On the way to transformation, the organization followed continuous delivery practice and invested in automation (major focus on automated testing). This resulted in multiple fold increase in time invested in developing new features or innovation.

Trunk Development

A model, where developers' works on software code in a single branch called 'trunk' and they resist creating other long standing development branches by practicing techniques. They avoid any merger step and do not break the continuity.

93

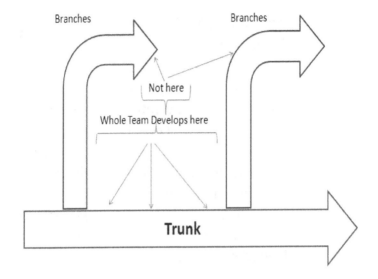

Practically, developers work in small high performing teams and develop off the trunk (on branches). The pragmatic way for best delivery performance could be:

- Daily merger of code into trunk.
- Branches with day log or less lifetimes
- Three or less active branches.

DevOps Architecture (Loosely Coupled)

Continuous delivery is driven greatly by the team and architecture which are loosely coupled. Loosely coupled team can complete their tasks independently. Similarly, loosely coupled architecture is the one where any modification can be done in the individual component or service without making changes in the dependent services or components.

The loosely coupled architecture results in strong IT and organizational performance because the delivery team can perform testing and deployment without depending on other teams for any work or approvals. It also avoids back- and – forth communication, making the process smooth and efficient.

Overall, it can be stated that more than automation of test and deployment process; the flexibility provided by loosely coupled architecture contributes towards continuous delivery.

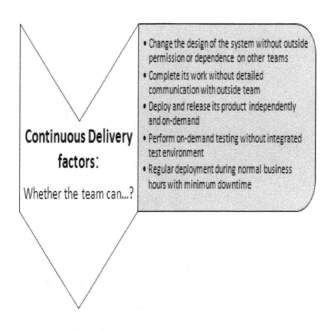

Continuous Delivery factors:

Whether the team can...?

- Change the design of the system without outside permission or dependence on other teams
- Complete its work without detailed communication with outside team
- Deploy and release its product independently and on-demand
- Perform on-demand testing without integrated test environment
- Regular deployment during normal business hours with minimum downtime

Emerging Trends in DevOps

1. **Containers and Micro services would be integrated**

big time with DevOps: "One of the major factors impacting DevOps is the shift towards micro services," says Arvind Soni, VP of product at Netsil

✓ **Microservices:** It is a application development architecture where applications are developed independently and are deployable, modular and small. Also, each modular service runs unique process and communicates in a defined manner serving business goals.

✓ **Containers:** It is an operating system virtualization method that facilitates application to run in resource isolated process. So, the application is deployed quickly, reliably and consistently in any deployment environment.

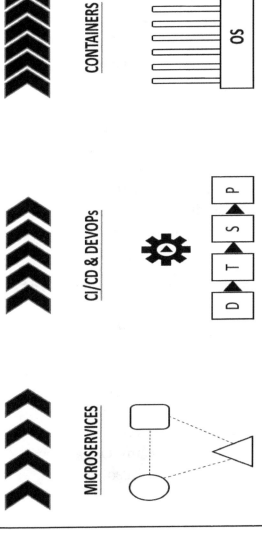

MICROSERVICES

SOFTWARE ARCHITECTURE
FOR GRANULAR DELIVERY

CI/CD & DEVOPs

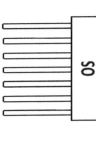

| D | T | S | P |

AUTOMATION OF DEV, TEST,
STAGE, PROD FOR SPEED/SCALE

CONTAINERS

OS

LIGHTWEIGHT & CONSISTENT APP
DELIVERY FOR SUREFIRE & SPEED

2. **Expert teams practicing DevOps would cut down on security nets**: It may be the case that expert DevOps teams may decide to no longer have pre-production environment. The team may be confident and the process of deploying and testing in staging environment may be avoided. Again this may be the case with expert teams who are confident to **identify, monitor** and resolve issues on production.

3. **Spread and integration of DevOps:** More frequent usage of the term "DevSecOps," reflects the intentional and much early inclusion of security aspect in the software development lifecycle. DevOps is also expected to expand into areas such as database teams, QA, and even outside of IT also.

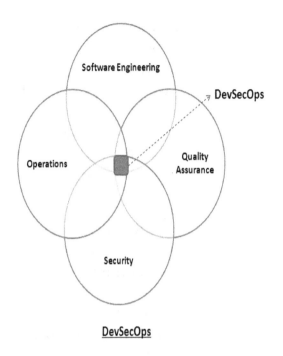

DevSecOps

4. **Increase in ROI**: As we move ahead in the DevOps way of application development IT teams would be more efficient and methodologies, processes, containers and micro services would contribute into higher ROI."The Holy Grail was to be moving faster, accomplishing

more and becoming flexible. As these components find broader adoption and organizations become more vested in their application the results shall appear," says Eric Schabell, global technology evangelist director, Red Hat.

5. **Evolution of success metrics:** On the path to DevOps evolution few points regarding the performance measurement matrices have been realized:
   ✓ Too many metrics to be avoided
   ✓ DevOps metrics should point out what's most important to you
   ✓ Business outcome relationship of the metrics are the key to standardization

Few of the DevOps metrics that may be relevant for the organization may be:

   ✓ Customer ticket volume
   ✓ % of successful deployment

- ✓ Job satisfaction of the deployment team
- ✓ % increase in time for innovation or adding new features

Overall, it is expected that all stakeholder would come together including security and database teams. The frictions caused by these teams would propel the number of releases exponentially.

Chapter 9 – DevOps Success Stories

Amazon is probably the most recognizable DevOps success story because simply put, it's one of the biggest and most recognizable companies in the world. Prior to implementing DevOps, Amazon was still running on dedicated servers. That practice made it very challenging to predict the amount of equipment they need to procure just to be able to meet website traffic demands. In an effort to minimize risks of being unable to meet those demands, Amazon had to pad their equipment requirement estimates just to have leeway for unusual or unexpected spikes in website traffic, which led to excess server capacity, i.e., server capacity wastage of up to 40%. And during shopping seasons like Christmas, up to 75% of server capacity was left unutilized. Economically, that was a very bad proposition.

Amazon's DevOps journey started when it transitioned to the AWS or Amazon Web Services Cloud. This allowed Amazon's engineers to incrementally scale capacity up or down as the need arose and let to substantial reductions in server capacity expenses. It also allowed Amazon to continuously deploy code – DevOps nirvana – to servers that needed new code whenever they want to.

Within 12 months from moving to AWS, Amazon's engineers were able to deploy code every 12 seconds or less on average. By switching to an Agile approach, Amazon was able to bring down significantly both the frequency and duration of website outages, which in turn increased its revenues.

Another very popular DevOps success story is **Wal-Mart** – the undisputed king of American big-box retail. While it's the undisputed king in physical shopping, it always lagged and struggled behind Amazon. In an effort to cut

Amazon's lead and gain much needed online ground, the company put together a very good team by acquiring several tech firms en route to establishing its own technology and innovation arm in 2011, WalmartLabs.

Through WalmartLabs, the parent company purposefully took a DevOps approach to establishing a powerful online presence. The technology and innovation subsidiary incorporated a cloud-based technology called OneOps, which automated and hastened the deployment of apps. Also, it came up with a couple of open source tools like Hapi, which is a Node.js framework that's used to build services and apps that in turn allowed the company's software developers to putting much of their effort and attention on programming multiple-use application logic. In turn, such application logic reduced the amount of time needed for building infrastructure.

By implementing DevOps, Wal-Mart was able to follow in the heels of Amazon.com and has substantially increased its revenues by foraging into the online market segment.

The most popular company that has successfully implemented DevOps is **Facebook.** The social media site practically changed the way the software industry thought about software development. Much of the initial principles it subscribed to in the beginning – including continuous improvements, automation, incremental changes, and code ownership – were considered to be DevOps by nature. Over the years, Facebook's approach has evolved, which has hastened its development lifecycle. In turn, the faster cycle continues to change the way people think about software. By being able to continuously deliver new updates to its app, Facebook continues to make people's experience in the social media platform even more fun, entertaining, and even addictive. It just gets better and better. And in doing so, Facebook was able to grow its business by leaps and bounds to the point where it became one of the biggest publicly listed companies in the New York Stock Exchange, the world's biggest stock market by capitalization. Below are the few latest examples of successful DevOps implementation:

Capital One's DevOps Success: Capital One is one of the largest digital bank in the world and it has been around for 20 years now. Capital One made a shift by adopting DevOps methodology to cater to growing requirements of Digital Banking Services. The approach changed when the engineers instead of writing codes for software and handing it to production team for testing ,fixing and pushing it to production worked together to complete the process using micro services and containers. They utilized the AWS cloud for running applications so that the IT team could focus on building digital products of highest quality.

Their team also insists the inclusion of databases in the DevOps adoption framework. This adoption makes databases respond much quickly to any change and saves time and provides return on investment.

American Airlines DevOps Success: After the acquisition of US Airways in 2013, the two IT teams decided to adopt DevOps as their answer their integration and roadmap issues. It became an opportunity to drive a cultural change at the organization. The two teams working in tandem led to creation of new applications and improved coordinated working culture.

Adobe's DevOps Success: When the organization moved from packaged software to cloud model, it was required to make series of small software updates rather than traditional annual releases. This led to adoption of DevOps methodology to meet the required pace of automating and managing the deployments. This move resulted in better and faster delivery and product management.

Netflix DevOps Success: Since Netflix entered into uncharted territory of streamlining videos instead of shipping DVD's, it required disruptive technologies to sustain its business. Today, the rate at which Netflix has adopted and implemented new technologies through DevOps approach is setting new bars in IT.

Major Success Stories

Conclusion

Thank you for buying this book. I hope that through this, you've become familiar with DevOps and Continuous Delivery and how they can help you grow your business. But as the saying goes, knowing is only half the battle and, in this case, the battle for growing your business. The other half is action. As such, I highly recommend that you act on the general knowledge you've gained about DevOps and CD through this book by reading more advanced material on the topic.

I would really appreciate if you can leave your review/feedback on the purchasing portal.

Here's to DevOps and Continuous Delivery for your business success my friend. Cheers!

Stephen Fleming

My Other Books available across the platforms in e-book, paperback and audible versions:

1. Blockchain Technology : Introduction to Blockchain Technology and its impact on Business Ecosystem

2. DevOps Handbook: Introduction to DevOps and its impact on Business Ecosystem

3. Blockchain Technology & DevOps: Introduction and impact on Business Ecosystem

4. Love Yourself: 21 day plan for learning "Self-Love" to cultivate self-worth ,self-belief, self-confidence & happiness

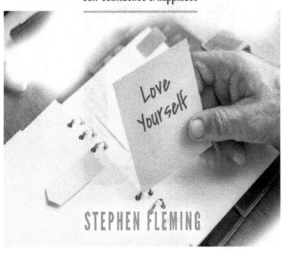

LOVE YOURSELF

21 day plan for learning "Self Love"
to cultivate self-worth, self-belief,
self-confidence & happiness

STEPHEN FLEMING

5. Intermittent Fasting: 7 effective techniques of Intermittent Fasting

7 EFFECTIVE TECHNIQUES OF

INTERMITTENT FASTING

Stay Healthy,Lose Weight,
Slow Down Aging Process & Live Longer!

STEPHEN FLEMING

** If you prefer audible versions of these books, I have few free coupons, drop me a mail at: **valueadd2life@gmail.com**. If available, I would mail you the same.

Book 2: Microservices Architecture Handbook

Non-Programmer's Guide for Building Microservices

BONUS MICROSERVICES BOOKLET

Dear Friend,

I am privileged to have you onboard. You have shown faith in me and I would like to reciprocate it by offering the maximum value with an amazing gift. I have been researching on the topic and have an excellent "Microservices Booklet" for you to take your own expedition on the subject to next level.

- Do you want to know the best online courses to begin exploring the topic?
- Do you want to know major success stories of Microservices implementation?
- What are the latest trends and news?

Also, do you want once in a while updates on interesting implementation of latest Technology; especially those impacting lives of common people? "Get Instant Access to Free Booklet and Future Updates"

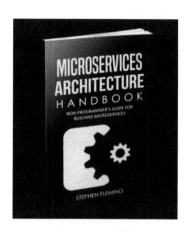

Type Link:
http://eepurl.com/ds8sfD

or

QR Code : You can download a QR code reader app on your mobile and open the link by scnning below:

Contents

Introduction

As the disruption of technologies continues to play a role in our lives, the application development process is becoming more flexible and agile. You must have heard about the concepts of Agile, DevOps, Kanban and many more. All these terminologies are basically making the application of development or the program writing exercise more flexible, more independent, and faster.

The Microservices architecture develops an application as a collection of loosely coupled services which is meant for different business requirements. Therefore, this architecture supports the continuous delivery/deployment of large, complex applications. It also enables the organization to evolve its application development capabilities.

Who can use this book?

This book can be used by a beginner, Technology Consultant, Business Consultant and Project Manager who are not directly into coding. The structure of the book is such that it answers the most asked questions about Microservices. It also covers the best and the latest case studies with benefits. Therefore, it is expected that after going through this book, you can discuss the topic with any stakeholder and take your agenda ahead as per your role. Additionally, if you are new to the industry, and looking for an application development job, this book will help you to prepare with all the relevant information and understanding of the topic.

Chapter 1: Monolith and Microservices

Microservices

In May 2011, a workshop of software architects was held in Venice and coined the term "Microservices" to relate to an upcoming software architectural technique that many of the software architectures had been researching. It wasn't until May 2012that Microservices was approved to be the most appropriate term to describe a style of software development. The first case study relating to Microservices architecture was presented by James Lewis in March, 2012, at the 33rd Degree in Krakow in Microservices-Java the Unix way. To date, numerous presentations about Microservices have been made at various conferences worldwide, with software architects presenting different designs and software components of Microservices and its integration to different platforms

128

and interfaces, such as Microsoft architecture and URI interface. Currently, Microservices has grown incredibly and has become an ideal way of developing small business applications, thanks to its efficiency and scalability. This software development technique is particularly perfect for developing software or applications compatible with a range of devices, both developed and yet to be developed, and platforms.

Microservices Defined

A standard definition of Microservices is not yet available, but it can be described as a technique of software application development which entails developing a single application as a suite of independently deployable, small, modular service. Every service controls processes and communicates with each other through a well-defined, lightweight mechanism, often as HTTP

129

resource API to serve a business goal. Microservices are built around business capabilities and are independently deployable by a fully automated deployment mechanism. They can be written in different programming languages such, as Java and C++ and employ different data storage technologies to be effective in the central management of enterprises or small businesses.

Microservices communicate to one other in several ways based on the requirements of the application employed in its development. Many developers use HTTP/REST with JSON or Protobuf for efficient communication. To choose the most suitable communication protocol, you must be a DevOps professional, and in most situations, REST (Representation State Transfer) communication protocol is preferred due to its lower complexity compared to other protocols.

Monolith Defined

A monolith is a software application whose modules cannot be executed independently. Thismakes monoliths difficult to use in distributed systems without specific frameworks or ad hoc solutions, such as Network Objects, RMI or CORBA. However, even these approaches still endure the general issues that affect monoliths, as discussed below.

Problems of Monoliths

1. Large-size monoliths are hard to maintain and evolve due to their complexity. Finding bugs requires long perusals through their code base.

2. Monoliths also suffer from the "dependency hell," in which adding or updating libraries results in inconsistent systems that either do not compile/run or, worse, misbehave.

3. Any change in one module of a

monolith requires rebooting the whole application. For large projects, restarting usually entails considerable downtimes, hindering the development, testing, and maintenance of the project.

4. Deployment of monolithic applications is usually suboptimal due to conflicting requirements on the constituent models' resources: some can be memory-intensive, others computational-intensive and others require ad hoc components (e.g. SQL-based, rather than graph-based databases). When choosing a deployment environment, the developer must compromise with a one-size-fits-all configuration, which is either expensive or suboptimal with respect to the individual modules.

5. Monoliths limit scalability. The usual strategy for handling increments of inbound requests is to create new instances of the same application

and to split the load amongst said instances. Moreover, it could be the increased traffic stresses only a subset of the modules, making the allocation of the newer resources for the other components inconvenient.

6. Monoliths also represent a technology lock-in for developers, which are bound to use the same language and frameworks of the original application

7. The Microservices architectural style has been proposed to cope with such problems as discussed above.

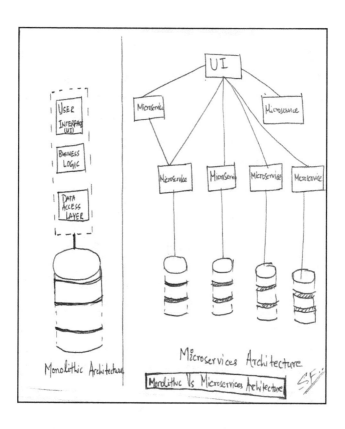

User Interface (UI)

Business Logic

Data Access Layer

Monolithic Architecture

UI

Microservice

Microservice

Microservice

MicroService

Microservice

Microservice

Microservices Architecture

Monolithic Vs Microservices Architecture

Future of Microservices

Over the years, software application development has evolved from Service-Oriented Architecture (SOA) to monolith architecture and now microservices architecture, which is the most preferred software application technique. Global organizations such as Amazon, eBay, Twitter, PayPal, The Guardian, and many others have not only migrated but also embraced microservices over SOA and Monolith architectures in developing their websites and applications. Will Microservices be the future of software application development? Time will tell.

Microservices compared to SOA

Microservices vs. SOA has generated lots of debate amongst software application developers, with some arguing that microservices is simply a refined improved version of SOA, while others consider microservices as a whole new concept in software application development which does not relate in any way with SOA. Nonetheless, microservices have a lot of similarities to SOA. The main difference between SOA and microservices may be thought to lie in the size and scope as suggested by the term "micro, "meaning small. Therefore, microservices are significantly smaller compared to SOA, and are deployed as an independent single unit. Furthermore, an SOA entails either numerous microservices or a single monolith. This debate can be concluded by referring to SOA as a relative of microservices. Nevertheless, they all perform the same role of software programme development, albeit in different ways.

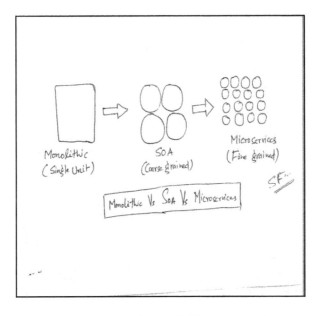

Features of Microservices Architecture

The features of microservices architecture differs widely as not all microservices have the same properties. However, we have managed to come up with several features that may be deemed appropriate and repetitive in almost all microservices.

Independent Deployment

Microservices are autonomous and can be deployed separately, making them less likely to cause system failures. This is done using components, which are defined as a unit of software that is independently replaceable and upgradeable. In addition to components, microservices architecture utilizes libraries or services. Libraries are components attached to a program using in-memory function calls. On the other hand, services are out-of-process components that communicate through different mechanisms, such as web service request mechanism Microservices applications. Software componentization involves breaking them into miniature components, termed as services. A good microservices architecture uses services as components rather than libraries, since they are independently deployable. An application consisting of multiple libraries cannot be deployed separately in a single process, since a single change to any component results in development and deployment of the entire application. An application consisting of multiple services is flexible and only a service is redeployed, rather than the entire application from a change in numerous service changes. It is therefore advantageous over library components.

Decentralized Data Management

This is a common feature in most Microsystems and involves the centralization of conceptual models and data storage decisions. This feature has been praised by small business enterprises, since a single database stores data from essentially all applications. Furthermore, each service manages its own database through a technique called Polyglot Persistence. Decentralization of data is also key in managing data updates in microservices systems. This guarantees consistency when updating multiple resources. Microservices architecture requires transactionless coordination between services to ensure consistency, since distributed transactions may be difficult to implement. Inconsistency in data decentralization is prevented through compensating operations. However, this may be difficult to manage. Nonetheless, inconsistency in data decentralization should be present for a business to respond effectively to real-time demand for their products or services. The cost of fixing inconsistencies is less compared to loss in a business experiencing great consistency in their data management systems.

Decentralized Governance

The microservices key feature is decentralized governance. The term governance means to control how people and solutions function to achieve organizational objectives. In SOA, governance guides the development of reusable service, developing and designing services, and establishing agreements between service providers and consumers. In microservices, architecture governance has the following capabilities;

- There is no need for central design governance, since microservices can make their own decisions concerning its design and implementation

- Decentralized governance enables microservices to share common and reusable services

- Some of the run-time governance aspects, such as SLAs, throttling, security monitoring and service discovery, may be implemented at the API-GW level, which we are going to discuss later

Service Registry and Service Discovery

Microservices architecture entails dealing with numerous microservices, which dynamically change in location owing to their rapid development/deployment nature.

141

Therefore, to find their location during a runtime, service registry and discovery are essential.

Service registry holds the microservices instance and their location. Microservices instance is registered with the service registry on start-up and deregistered on shutdown. Clients can, therefore, find available services and their location through a service location

Service discovery is also used to find the location of an available service. It uses two mechanisms, i.e. Client-Side Discovery and Service-Side Discovery

Advantages of Microservices

Microservices comes with numerous advantages, as discussed below:

Cost effective to scale

You don't need to invest a lot to make the entire application scalable. In terms of a shopping cart, we could simply load balance the product search module and the order-processing module while leaving out less frequently used operation services, such as inventory management, order cancellation, and delivery confirmation.

Clear code boundaries

This action should match an organization's departmental hierarchies. With different departments sponsoring product development in large enterprises, this can be a huge advantage.

Easier code changes

The code is done in a way that it is not dependent on the code of other modules and is only achieving isolated functionality. If it is done right, the chances of a change in microservices affecting other microservices are very minimal.

Easy deployment

Since the entire application is more like a group of ecosystems that are isolated from each other, deployment could be done one microservices at a time, if required. Failure in any one of these would not bring the entire system down.

Technology adaptation

You could port a single microservices or a whole bunch of them overnight to a different technology without your users even knowing about it. And yes, hopefully, you don't expect us to tell you that you need to maintain those service contracts, though.

Distributed system

This comes as implied, but a word of caution is necessary here. Make sure that your asynchronous calls are used well, and synchronous ones are not really blocking the whole flow of information. Use data partitioning well. We will come to this a little later, so don't worry for now.

Quick market response

The world being competitive is a definite advantage; otherwise, users tend to quickly lose interest if you are slow to respond to new feature requests or adoption of a new technology within your system.

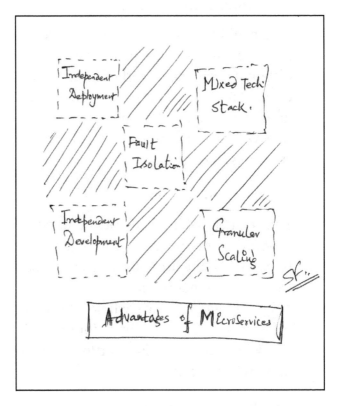

Chapter 2: Understanding Microservices Architecture

Microservices have different methods of performing their functions based on their architectural style, as a standard microservices model does not exist. To understand microservices architecture, we should first analyze it in terms of service, which can be described as the basic unit in microservices. As briefly defined in chapter 1, Services are processes that communicate over a network to fulfill a goal using technology-agnostic protocols such as HTTP. Apart from technologic-agnostic protocols as a means of communication over a network, services also utilize other means of inter-process communication mechanisms, such as a shared memory for efficient communication over networks. Software developed through microservices architecture technique can be broken down into multiple component services. Each of the components in a service can be deployed, twisted according to the developer's specifications and then independently redeployed without having to develop an entirely new software application. However, this technique has its disadvantages, such as expensive remote calls, and complex procedures when redeploying and redistributing responsibilities between service components.

Services in microservices are organized around business capabilities such as user interface, front-end, recommendation, logistics, billing etc. The services in microservices can be implemented using different programming languages, databases, hardware, and software environments, depending on the developer's preferences. Microservices utilizes the cross-functional team, unlike a traditional monolith development approach where each team has a specific focus on technology layers, databases,

Uls, server-side logic or technology layers. Each team in microservices is required to implement specific products based on one or more individual service communicating via a message bus. This improves the communicability of microservices over a network between a business enterprise and the end users of their products. While most software development technique focuses on handing a piece of code to the client and in turn maintained by a team, microservices employs the use of a team who owns a product for a lifetime.

A microservices based architecture adheres to principles such as fine-grained interface, business-driven development, IDEAL cloud application architectures, polyglot programming and lightweight container deployment and DevOps with holistic service monitoring to independently deploy services. To better our understanding of microservices, we can relate it to the classic UNIX system, i.e. they receive a user request, process them, and generate a response based on the query generated. Information flows in a microsystem through the dump pipes after being processed by smart endpoints.

Microservices entails numerous platforms and technologies to effectively execute their function. Microservices developers prefer to use decentralized governance over centralized governance, as it provides them with developing tools which can be used by other developers to solve emerging problems in software application development. Unlike microservices, monoliths systems utilize a single logical database across different platforms with each service managing its unique database.

The good thing about microservices is that it's a dynamic evolutionary software application technique in software application development. Therefore, it's an evolutionary design system which is ideal for the development of timeless applications which is compatible through future technologically sophisticated devices. In summary, Microservices functions by using services to componentized software applications, thereby ensuring efficient communication between applications and users over a network to fulfill an intended goal. The services are fine-grained and the protocols lightweight to break applications into small services to improve modularity and enable users to easily understand the functionality, development, and testing of the application software.

How Microservices Architecture Functions

Just like in programming, microservices have a wide range of functionality depending on the developer's choice. Microservices architecture functions by structuring applications into components or libraries of loosely coupled services, which are fine-grained and the protocols lightweight. But to understand its functionality, we should first look at Conway's law.

Conway's Law

A computer programmer named Melvin Conway came up a law in 1967 which states that "organizations which design system...are constrained to produce designs which are copies of the communication structure of these organization". This means that for a software module to function effectively there should be frequent communication between the authors. Social boundaries within an organization are reflected through the software interface structure within the application. Conway's law is the basic principle of the functionality of microservices and highlights the dangers of trying to enforce an application design that does not match the organizational requirements. To understand this, let's use an example: an organization having two departments i.e. accounting and customer support departments, whose application system are obviously interconnected. A problem arises that the accounting is overworked and cannot handle numerous tasks of processing both dissatisfied customer refunds and credit their accounts while the customer support department is underworked and very idle. How can the organization solve this problem? This is where microservices architecture comes in! The roles and responsibilities of each department in the interconnected system are split accordingly to improve customer satisfaction and minimize business losses in the organization.

In splitting the roles and responsibilities of each department, Interface Separation Principle is essential when implementing microservices to solve this problem. A typical approach isolating issues of concern in an organization through microservices is to find a communication point in the software application, then link the application by drawing a "dotted line" between the two halves of the system. However, this technique, if not carefully carried out, leads to smaller growing monoliths, which leads to isolation of important codes on the wrong side of the barrier.

Avoiding Monoliths in Microservices architecture application

Accidental monoliths are common problems when developing software applications using microservices architecture. An application may become infected with unhealthy interdependencies when service boundaries are blurred, and one service can start using the data source interface of another or even for code related to a certain logic or function to be spread over multiple places due to accidental monoliths which grow with time. This can be avoided by establishing the edge of developed application software graph.

Key Points in the Working of Microservices Architecture

- Its programming of the modern

era, where we are expected to follow the SOLID principles. It's object-oriented programming (OOP).

- It is the best way to expose the functionality of other or external components in a way that any other programming language will be able to use the functionality without adhering to any specific user interfaces, that is, services (web services, APIs, rest services, and so on).

- The whole system works according to a type of collaboration that is not interconnected or interdependent.

- Every component is liable for its own responsibilities. In other words, components are responsible for only one functionality.

- It segregates code with a separation concept, and the segregated code is reusable.

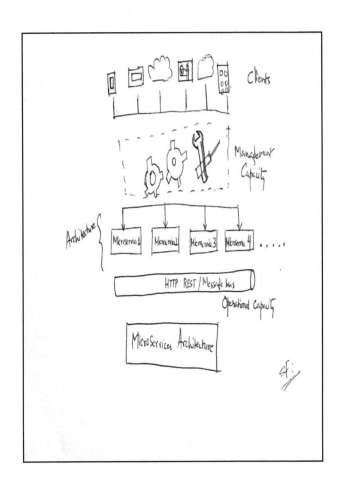

Clients

Management Capacity

Architecture {

| Microservice 1 | Microservice 2 | Microservice 3 | Microservice 4 | . . . . .

HTTP REST / Message bus

Operational Capacity

MicroServices Architecture

155

Chapter 3: Building Microservices

We have introduced and described the functionality of microservices. In this chapter, we are going to discuss how to build microservices by separating them from the existing system and creating separate services for products and orders which can be deployed independently. First, we will begin by discussing the core concepts, programming languages, and tools that can be used to build microservices.

C#

In 2002, Microsoft developed the C# programming language and the latest release is the C# 7.0. C# is an object-oriented language and component oriented, with features like Deconstructors, ValueTuple, pattern matching, and much more.

Java Programming Language

Java is a general-purpose programming language that is concurrent, class-based, object-oriented and designed to have few implementation dependencies as possible to let application developers "write once, run anywhere" (WORA), meaning that it can run on all platforms that support Java.

Entity Framework Core

Entity framework core is a cross-platform version of Microsoft Entity Framework and can be used as a tool to build microservices. It is one of the most popular object-relational mappers (ORMs). ORM can be defined as a technique to query and manipulate data as per required business output.

.Net Framework

Developed by Microsoft, .NetFramework is a software framework that runs on Microsoft Windows with Framework Class Library to provide language interoperability across several programming languages. Programs are written for .NET Framework execute software environment, rather than hardware environment, or Common Language Runtime(CLR)

Visual Studio 2017

Visual Studio 2017 is an Integrated Development Environments (IDE) developed by Microsoft to enable software application developers to build applications using various programming languages, such as Java, C#, and many more.

Microsoft SQL Server

Microsoft SQL Server(MSSQL) is a software application that has a relational database software management system which is used to store and retrieve data as requested by other software applications. It can be used in the management of microservices and it is able to communicate across a network.

Aspects of Building Microservices

To build microservices, we should first look at the important aspects, such as size and services to ensure their effective functionality after separating them from the main system.

Size of microservices

In building microservices, the first step is to break or decompose applications or systems into smaller segments or functionalities of the main application known as services. Factors to consider for high-level isolation of microservices are discussed below.

Risk due to requirement changes

It is important to note that a change in one microservice should be independent of the other microservices. Therefore, software should be isolated into smaller components termed as services in a way that if there are any requirement changes in one service, they should be independent from other microservices.

Changes in Functionality

In building microservices, we isolate functionalities that are rarely changed from the dependent functionalities that can be frequently modified. For example, in our application, the customer module notification functionality will rarely change. But its related modules, such as Order, are more likely to have frequent business changes as part of their life cycle.

Team changes

We should also consider isolating modules in such a way that one team can work independently of all the other teams. If the process of making a new developer productive—regarding the tasks in such modules—is not dependent on people outside the team, it means we are well placed.

Technology changes

Technology use needs to be isolated vertically within each module. A module should not be dependent on a technology or component from another module. We should strictly isolate the modules developed in different technologies, or stacks, or look at moving them to a common platform as the last resort.

In building microservices, the primary goal is to isolate services from the main application system and keep it as small as possible.

Features of a good Service

A good service is essential in the buildingof a good microservices architecture. A good service that can be easily used and maintained by developers and users should have the following characteristics.

Standard Data Formats

A good service should follow standardized data formats, while exchanging services or systems with other components. Most popular data formats used in the.Netstack are XML and JSON

161

Standard communication protocol

Good services should adhere to standard communication formats such as SOAP and REST.

Loose coupling

Coupling refers to the degree of direct knowledge that one service has of another. Therefore, loosely coupled means that they should not have little knowledge of the other service, so that a change in one service will not impact the other service.

Domain -Driven Design in building Microservices

Domain-Driven Design (DDD) is a technique in designing complex systems and can be useful in designing and building microservices. DDD can be described as a blueprint used to build microservices and, once it's done, a microservices can implement it just the way an application implements, let's say, an order service or an inventory service.

The main principle in domain design is to draft a model which can be written in any programming language after understanding an exact domain problem. A domain driven model, should be reusable, loosely coupled, independently designed, and should be easily isolated from a software application without having to deploy a new system.

After building microservices from a domain-based model. It is important to ensure that the size of the microservices is small enough. This can be done by having a baseline for the maximum number of domain objects which can communicate to each other. You can also do this by verifying the size all interfaces and classes in each microservices. Another way of ensuring a small size of microservices is by achieving the correct vertical isolation of services. You can then deploy each of the services independently. By deploying each service independently, we allow the host in an application to perform its independent process which is beneficial in harnessing the power of the cloud and other hybrid models of hosting.

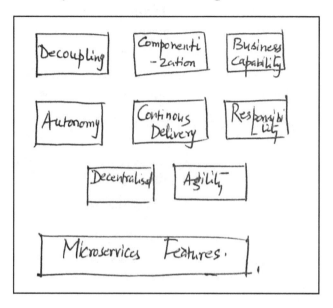

Building Microservices from Monolithic Application

As discussed earlier, the functionality in microservices lies in the isolation of services from the rest of application system translating into advantages discussed in *chapter 1* such as code reusability, independent deployment and easier code maintenance. Building microservices from monolithic application needs thorough planning. Many software architects have different approaches when it comes to transiting from monoliths to microservices, but the most important thing to consider is a correct method, as there is a possibility microservices failing to carry out their function when translated from monolith application using a wrong method. Some of the factors to consider when building microservices from the monolithic application are discussed below:

Module interdependency

When building microservices from the monolithic application, the starting point should always be to identify and pick up those parts of the monolithic application that are least dependent on other modules and have the least dependent on them. This part of the application is essential in identifying isolating application codes from the rest of the system, thereby becoming a part of the microservices which are then deployed independently in the final stage of the process. This small part of the application is referred as seams.

Technology

Technology in the form of an application's base framework is important in achieving this process. Before choosing a software framework, such as the ones discussed in this chapter, you should first identify their features. Building microservices is heavily dependent on data structures, inter-process communication being performed, and the activity of report generation. In this regard, a developer should therefore choose a framework that has great features and is ahead in technology, as they enable them to perform the transition correctly

Team structure

Team structure is important in the transition, as they are the workforce in building microservices. Teams greatly differ based on the geographical location, security of the company, and their technical skills. For the team to optimize their productivity in building microservices, they should be able to work independently. Furthermore, the team should safeguard the intellectual property of the company in developing a microservices based application.

Database

The database is considered the biggest asset of a system and their domain is defined by database tables and stored procedure. Contrary to most misconceptions, building microservices from the monolithic application does not involve dividing the whole database at once, but rather a step-by-step procedure. First, a database structure used to interact with the database is identified. Then the database structure is isolated into separate codes, which are then aligned with the newly defined vertical boundaries. Secondly, the underlying database structure is broken using the same method as the first step. The database change should not define the module used in the transition to microservices-style architecture, but rather the module should define the database. The database structure should relate to the modules picked in the transition to ensure ease in building microservices.

It is important to understand the types of acceptable changes in breaking down and merging a database, as not all changes can be implemented by the system due to data integrity. When restructuring a database to match the microservices architecture, removing foreign key relationship is the most important step, as microservices are designed to function independently of other services in an application. The

168

final step in breaking database in microservices-style architecture is isolating the ORDER table from the ProductID, as they are still sharing information, i.e. loose coupling.

In summary, breaking down a database in microservices architecture style involves two important steps: Isolating the data structures in the code and removing foreign key relationships. It is important to note that splitting the database is not the final step in building microservices from monolithic applications, as there are other steps.

Transaction

After splitting the database from the steps mentioned above, the next step is to link services to the database in a way that ensures data integrity is maintained. However, not all services successfully go through a transaction to their successful databases due to several reasons, such as a communication fault within the system or insufficient quantities for the product requested in e-commerce platforms. For example, Amazon and e-commerce. These problems can be solved by orchestrating the whole transaction, record individual transactions across the service, or to cancel the entire transaction across the services in the system. However, when the transactions are planned out well in a microservices-style architecture application, this problem can beavoided

Building Microservices with Java

Building microservices in a java ecosystem includes container-less, self-contained and in-container strategies, all of which are discussed below.

Container-less microservices

Container-less microservices package the application, with all of its dependencies, into a single JAR file. This approach is very advantageous, due to the ease of starting and stopping services as necessary in scaling. A JAR file is also conveniently passed around by the team members that need it.

Self-contained microservices

Like container-fewer microservices, microservices are packaged into a single fat JAR file with the inclusion of embedded framework with optional compatible third-party libraries, such as Wildfly Swarm and Spring Boot, both of which will be discussed later in this chapter.

In-Container microservices

In-container microservices package an entire Java EE container and its service implementation in a Docker image. The container provides verified implementations through standard APIs, giving the developer the opportunity to solely focus on business functionality.

Microservices Framework for Java

Apart from the containers discussed above, building microservices in Java entails several microservices frameworks, such as Spring Boot, Jersey, Swagger, Dropwizard, Ninja

Web Framework, Play Framework, and many more. We are going to handle just a few common microservices frameworks below.

Microservices in Spring Boot

Spring Boot is one of the best microservices frameworks, since it is optimally integrated with supporting languages. You can Spring Boot on your own device via an embedded server. Spring Boot also eliminates the necessity of using Java EE containers.This is enabled through the implementation of Tomcat. Spring boot projects include:

Spring IO Platform: An enterprise-grade distribution for versioned applications.

Spring Framework: Used for transaction management, data access, dependency injection, messaging, and web apps.

Spring Cloud: Used for distributed systems and also used for building or deploying your microservices.

Spring Data: Used for microservices that are related to data access, be it map-reduce, relational or even non-relational.

Spring Batch: Used for higher levels of batch operations.

Spring Security: Used for authorization and authentication support.

Spring REST Docs: Used for documenting RESTful services.

Spring Social: Used for connecting to social media APIs.

Spring Mobile: Used for mobile Web apps.

Microservices in Dropwizard

Dropwizard combines mature and stable Java libraries in lightweight packages for use in a certain application. It uses Jetty for HTTP, Jersey for REST, and Jackson for JSON, along with Metrics,

173

Guava, Logback, Hibernate Validator, Apache HTTP Client, Liquibase, Mustache, Joda Time, and Freemarker. Maven is used to set up Dropbox application, after which a configuration class, an application class, a representation class, a resource class, or a health check can be created to run the applications.

Jersey

Jersey is an open source framework based on JAX-RS specifications. Jersey's applications can extend existing JAX-RS implementations with more features and utilities to make RESTful services and client development simpler and easier. Jersey is fast and easily routed, coupled with great documentation filled with examples for easy practice.

Play Framework

Play Framework provides an easier way to build, create, and deploy Web applications using Scala and Java. It is ideal for REST application that requires parallel handling of remote calls. It is one of the most used microservices frameworks with modular, and supports async. An example of code in Play Framework is shown below.

Restlet

Restlet enables developers to create fast and scalable WEB APIs that adhere to the RESTful architecture pattern discussed above. It has good routing and filtering, and it's available for Java SE/EE, OSGi, Google AppEngine, Android, and other major platforms. However, learning Restlet can be difficult due to the small number of users and the unavailability of tutorials. An example of a code in Restlet is shown below.

Chapter 4: Integrating Microservices

Integrating microservices refers to interaction and communication of independent services located in a separate database within a software application. First, let us look at communication between microservices.

Communication between Microservices

Microservices communicate using an inter-process communication mechanism with two main message formats, namely binary and text. There are two kinds of inter-process communication mechanisms that microservices can be used to communicate, i.e. asynchronous messaging and synchronous request/response, both of which are discussed below.

Asynchronous Communication

This is an inter-process communication mechanism in which microservices communicate by asynchronously exchanging messages. It means that when an organizational client sends a message to a service to perform a certain task or answer a query, the service replies by sending a separate message back to the client. The messages, consisting of a title and body, are exchanged over channels with no limitation to the number of organizations and their clients sending and receiving messages. Likewise, any number of consumers can receive multiple messages from a single communication channel. There are two types of channels, namely: publish-subscribe and point-to-point channels. A point-to-point channel delivers a message to exactly one client reading from the channel, while the publish-subscribe channel delivers a common message to all the attached clients in a certain organization. Services utilize

177

point-to-point channel to communicate directly to clients and publish-subscribe communication to interact with one too many clients attached to an organization

For instance, when a client requests a trip through an application, The Trip Management is notified and in turn notifies the Dispatch department about the new trip through a Trip Created message to a publish-subscribe channel. The Dispatcher then locates an available driver and notifies them by writing a Driver Proposed message to a publish-subscribe channel.

Some of the advantages of this type of communication include message buffering, isolating the client from the service, flexibility in client-service interactions, and explicitly in inter-process communication. However, there are certain downsides, such as additional operational costs, since the system is a separate entity and must be installed, configured, and operated separately, and the complexity of implementing request/ response-based interaction.

Synchronous, Request/Response IPC Mechanism

In this inter-process mechanism, a client sends a request to a service, which in turn processes the request and sends back a response. The client believes that the response will arrive in a timely fashion. While using synchronous IPC mechanism, one can choose various protocols to choose from, but the most common ones are REST and Thrift, as discussed below.

REST

REST is an IPC mechanism that uses HTTP to communicate. The basic in REST is a resource which can be equated to a business entity, such as a product or a customer or a collection of business objects. REST utilizes HTTP verbs referenced using a URL to manipulate resources. The key benefit of using this protocol is that it's simple and familiar and supports request/response-style communication, thereby enabling real-time communication within an organization and numerous clients. Some of the drawbacks include that the intermediary and buffer messages must all run concurrently and that the client must know the location of each service through a URL.

Thrift

An alternative to REST is the Apache Thrift, which provides a C-style IDL for defining APIs. Thrift is essential in generating client-side stubs and server-side skeletons. A thrift interface is made up of one or more services, which can return a value to implement the request/response style of interaction. Thrift also supports various message formats such, as JSON, binary, and compact binary.

Integration Patterns

We have discussed communication between microservices through synchronous and asynchronous inter-process communication, but this alone does not guarantee integration, as integration patterns are also essential in their communication. We will discuss the implementation of various integration patterns required by an application.

The API Gateway

The API gatewaysits between clients and services by acting as a reverse proxy, routing requests from clients to services. It acts as a proxy between services and client applications. The Azure API management as an example is responsible for the following functionalities.

- Accepting API calls

- Verifying API keys, JWT tokens, and certificates

- Supporting Auth through Azure AD and OAuth 2.0 access token

- Enforcing usage quotas and rate

limits

- Caching backend responses

- Logging call metadata for analytics purposes

To understand the integration of microservices in Azure API gateway, let's use an example of an application split into microservices, namely product service, order service, invoice service, and customer service. In this application,the Azure API will be working as an API Gateway to connect clients to services. The API gateway enables clients to access services in servers unknown to them by providing its own server address and authenticating the client's request by using a valid *Ocp-Apim-Subscription-Key*

Different API commands execute certain functions in a service, as shown in the table below:

API Resource	Description
GET /api/product	Gets a list of products
GET /api/product/{id}	Gets a product
PUT /api/product/{id}	Updates an existing product
DELETE /api/product/{id}	Deletes an existing product
POST /api/product	Adds a new product

The Event-Driven pattern

A microservice has a database per service pattern, meaning that it has an independent database for every dependent or independent service. Dependent services require a few external services or components, and internal services to function effectively. Dependent service does not work if any or all the services on which the service is dependent on do not work properly. Independent service does not require any other service to work properly, as the name suggests.

In the diagram, the event-manager could be a program which runs on a service which enables it to manage all the events of the subscribers. Whenever a specific event is triggered in the Publisher, the event-manager notifies a Subscriber.

Event Sourcing

Event sourcing pattern enables developers to publish an event whenever the state changes. The EventStore persists the events available for subscription, or as other services. In this pattern, tasks are simplified to avoid additional requirements in synchronizing the data model and business domain, thereby improving responsiveness, scalability, and

184

responsiveness in the microservices. For example, in an application having ORDERSERVICE as the services, a command issues a book for the User Interface to be ordered. ORDERSERVICE queries and populates the results with the `CreateOrder` event from the Event Store. The command handler raises an event to order the book, initiating a related operation. Finally, the system authorizes the event by appending the event to the event store.

Compensating Transactions

Compensating transactions refers to a means used to undo tasks performed in a series of steps. For instance, a service has implemented operations in a series and one or more tasks have failed. Compensating transactions is used to reverse the steps in a series.

Competing Consumers

Competing consumers is essential in processing messages for multiple concurrent consumers to receive the messages on the same channel. It enables an application to handle numerous requests from clients. It is implemented by passing a messaging system to another service through asynchronous communication.

Azure Service Bus

Azure Service Bus is an information delivery service used to enhance communication between two or more services. Azure Service Bus can be described as a means through which services communicate or exchange information. Azure Service Bus provides two main types of service, which are broken and non-broken communication. Broken communication is a real-time communication that ensures communication between a sender or a receiver, even when they are offline. In non-broken communication, the sender is not informed whether information has been received or not by the receiver.

Azure queues

Azure queues are cloud storage accounts which use Azure Table. They provide a means to queue a message between applications.

In summary, integrating microservices is through communication between services. Microservices communicate through inter-service communication, which can be synchronous or asynchronous. In asynchronous inter-process communication, API gateway is used to allow clients to communicate to services by acting as an intermediary between clients and services. Microservices also communicate through various patterns, as discussed in the chapter.

Chapter 5: Testing Microservices

Testing microservices is an important way of ensuring their functionality by assessing the system, applications, or programs in different aspects to identify an erroneous code. Testing microservices varies in systems, depending on the microservices architectural style employed.

How to Test Microservices

It is easier to test a monolithic application than to test microservices, since monoliths provide implementation dependencies and short note delivery cycles. This is because testing microservices involves testing each service separately, with the test technique different for each service. Testing microservices can be challenging, since each service is designed to work independently.

Therefore, they are tested individually rather than as a whole system It gets more challenging when testing is combined with continuous integration and deployment. However, these challenges can be solved by using a unit test framework. For example, Microsoft Unit Testing Framework, which provides a facility to test individual operations of independent components. These tests are run on every compilation of the code to ensure success in the test.

Testing Approach

As mentioned above, different application systems require different testing approaches. The testing strategy should be unique to a system and should be clear to everyone, including the none technical members of a team. Testing can be manual or automated and should be simple to perform by a system user. Testing approaches have the following techniques.

Proactive Testing

A testing approach that tries to fix defects before a build is created from the initial test designs

Reactive Testing

Testing is started after the completion of coding.

Testing Pyramid

To illustrate testing microservices, we use the testing pyramid. The Testing pyramid showcases how a well-designed test strategy is structured.

Testing Pyramid:

- System Tests (Top)

- Service Tests (Middle)

- Unit Tests (Bottom)

Unit Test

Unit testing involves testing small functionalities of an application based on the microservices architectural style.

Service Tests

Service tests entail testing an independent service which communicates with another/external service

System Tests

They are end-to-end tests, useful in testing the entire system with an aspect of the user interface. System testsare expensive and slow to maintain and write, while service and unit testsare fast and less expensive.

Types of Microservices Test

There are various types of microservices test, as discussed below.

Unit Testing

Unit testing is used to test a single function in a service, thereby ensuring that the smallest piece of the program is tested. They are carried out to a verify a specific functionality in a system without having to test other components in the process. Unit testing is very complex, since the components are broken down into independent, small components that can be tested independently. A Test-Driven Development is used to perform a unit test.

Component (service) Testing

In service testing, the units(UI) are directly bypassed and the API, such as .Net Core Web API, is tested directly. Testing a service involves testing an independent service or a service interacting with an external device. A mock and stub approach is used to test a service interacting with an external service through an API gateway.

Integration Testing

Integration testing involves testing services in components working together. It is meant to ensure that the system is working together correctly as expected. For example, an application has StockService and OrderService depending on each other. Using integration testing, StockService is tested individually by ensuring it does not communicate with OrderService. This is accomplished through mock.

Contract Testing

Contract testing is a test that involves verifying response in each independent service. In this test, any service that is dependent on an external service is stubbed, therefore making it function independently. This test is essential in checking the contract of external services through consumer-driven contract, as discussed below.

Consumer-driven contracts

Consumer-driven refers to an integration pattern, which specifies and verifies interactions between clients and the application through the API gateway. It specifies the type of interactions a client is requesting with a defined format. The applications can then approve the requests through consumer-driven contract.

Performance Testing

It is a non-functional testing with the aim of ensuring the system is performing perfectly according to its features, such as scalability and reliability. Performance testing involves various techniques, as described below.

Load Testing

This technique involves testing the behavior of the application system under various conditions of a specific load, such as database load, critical transactions, and application servers

Stress Testing

It is a test where the system is exposed to regress stressing to find the upper capacity of the system. It is aimed at determining the behavior of a system in critical conditions, such as when the current load overrides the maximum load.

Soak Testing

Also called endurance testing, soak testing is aimed at monitoring memory utilization, memory leaks, and other factors influencing system performance

Spike Testing

Spike testing is an approach inwhich the system is tested to ensure it can sustain the workload. It can be done by suddenly increasing the workload and monitoring system performance

End-to-end (UI/functional) testing

UI test is performed on the whole system, including the entire service and database. This test is the highest level of testing in microservices and it's mainly performed to increase the scope of testing. It includes fronted integration.

Sociable versus isolated unit Tests

Sociable tests resemble system tests and are performed to ensure that the application is running smoothly and as expected. Additionally, it tests other

195

software in the same application environment. Isolated software, on the other hand, is performed before stubbing and mocking to perform unit testing, as discussed earlier. Unit testing can also be used to perform using stubs in concrete class

Stubs and Mocks

Stubs and mocks are the mockimplementations of objects interacting with the code when performing a test. The object can be replaced with a stub in one test and a mock on the other, depending on the intention of the test. Stubs can be referred to as inputs to the code under test, while mocks are outputs of a code under test

Summary

We have discussed that testing microservices is more challenging compared to testing monolithic applications in a .Net framework. The pyramid test concept enables us to

196

understand and strategize the testing procedures. Unit test is used in testing small functionalities and class in a microservices application. Tests on top of the pyramid, such as end-end testing, are used to test the entire microservices application, rather than small functionalities or services in the application.

Chapter 6: Deploying Microservices

Deploying microservices can also be challenging and is done through continuous integration and continuous deployment. Additionally, new technology such as toolchain technology and container technologies have proven essential in deploying microservices. In this chapter, we are going to discuss the basics of microservices deployment and the new technologies mentioned above. But first let's look at the key requirements in their deployment.

Deployment Requirement

- Ability to deploy/un-deploy services independent of other microservices

- A service must be able to, at each microservices level, ensure a given service does not receive more traffic compared to other services in the application.

- A failure in one microservices must not affect other services in the application

- Building and deploying microservices quickly

Designing Microservices — Best Practices

Steps in Microservices Deployment

In this section, we are going to discuss the first step, i.e. Build to the final stage, which is the release stage.

Build Stage

In the build stage, a docker container is made to provide the necessary tools to create the microservices. A second container is then applied to run the built container. Then, a service source is compiled carefully to prevent errors. The services are later tested using unit testing to ensure their correspondence. The final product in this stage is a build artifact.

Continuous Integration (CI)

Any changes in the microservices build the entire application through CI. This occurs because the application code gets compiled and a comprehensive set of automated tests are run against it. CI was developed due to the problem of frequent integration. The basic idea behind CI is to ensure small changes in the software application by preserving a Delta.

Deployment

Requirements for deployment include the hardware specifications, base OS, and the correct version of a software framework. The final part is to promote the build artifacts produced in the first stage. In microservices, there is a distinction between the deployment stage and the release stage.

Continuous Deployment (CD)

In this stage, each build is deployed to the production. It is important in the deployment of microservices, as it ensures that the changes pushed to production through various lower environment work as expected in the production. This stage involves several practices, such as automated unit testing, labeling, versioning of build numbers, and traceability of changes.

Continuous Delivery

Continuous delivery is different from continuous deployment(CD) and it's focused on providing the deployment code as early as possible to the customer. In Continuous Delivery, every build is passed through quality checks to prevent errors. Continuous Delivery is implemented through automation by the build and deployment pipeline. Build and deployment pipelines ensure that a code is committed in the source repository.

Release

This is the final stage in microservices deployment and involves making a service available to possible clients. The relevant build artifact is deployed before the release of a service managed by a toggle.

Fundamentals for Successful Microservices Deployment

For microservices to be deployed

successfully, the following things should be done.

Self-sufficient Teams

A team should have sufficient members with all the necessary skills and roles i.e. developers and analysts. A self-sufficient team will be able to handle development, operations, and management of microservices effectively. Smaller self-sufficient teams, who can integrate their work frequently, are precursors to the success of microservices.

CI and CD

CI and CD are essential in implementing microservices, as they automate the system to be able to push code upgrades regularly, thereby enabling the team to handle complexity by deploying microservices, as discussed above.

Infrastructure Coding

Infrastructure coding refers to representing hardware and

203

infrastructure components, such as network servers into codes. It is important to provide deployment environments to make integration, testing, and build production possible in microservices production. It also enables developers to produce defects in lower environments. Tools such as CFEngine, Chef, Puppet, Ansible and PowerShell DSC can be used to code infrastructure. Through infrastructure coding, an infrastructure can be put under a version control system, then deployed as an artifact to enhance microservices deployment.

Utilization of Cloud Computing

Cloud computing is important in the adoption and deployment of microservices. It comes with near infinite scale, elasticity, and rapid provision capability. Therefore, it should be utilized to ensure successful deployment of microservices.

Deploying Isolated Microservices

In 2012, Adam Wiggins developed a set of principles known as a 12-factor app, which can be used to deploy microservices. According to the principles, the services are essentially stateless except for the database. These principles are applied in deploying isolated microservices as follows.

Service teams

The team should be self-sufficient and built around services. They should be able to make the right decision to develop and support microservices decision.

Source control isolation

Source control isolation ensures that microservices do not share any source code or files in their respiratory. However, codes can be duplicated to avoid this problem.

Build Stage Isolation

Build and deploy pipelines for

microservices should be isolated and separate. For isolated deployed services, build and deploy pipelines run separately. Due to this, the CI-CD tool is scaled to support different services and pipelines at a faster stage.

Release Stage Isolation

Every microservice is released in isolation with other services.

Deploy Stage Isolation

It is the most important stage in deploying isolated microservices.

Containers

Containers can be defined as pieces of software in a complete file system. Container technology is new and is now linked to the Linux world. Containers are essential in running code, runtime, system tools, and system libraries. They share their host operating system and kernel with other containers on the same host.

Deploying   Microservices   with Docker.

Docker is an open-source engine that lets developers and system administrators deploy self-sufficient application containers (defined above) in Linux environment. It is a great way to deploy microservices. The building deploying when starting microservices is much faster when using the Docker platform. Deploying microservices using docker is performed by following these simple steps.

- The microservices is packaged as a Docker container image

- Each service is deployed as a container

- Scaling is done based on changing the number of container instances.

Terminologies used in Docker

Docker image

A Docker image is a read-only template

containing instructions for creating a Docker container. It consists of a separate filesystem, associated libraries, and so on. It can be composed of layers on top each other, like a layered cake. Docker images used in different containers can be reused, thereby reducing the deployment footprints of applications using the same images. A Docker image can be stored at the Docker hub.

Docker registry

Docker registry is a library of images and can either be private or public. It can also be on the same server as the Docker daemon or Docker client, or on a totally different server.

Dockerfile

A Dockerfile is a scripted file containing instructions on how to build a Docker image. The instructions are in the form multiple steps, starting from obtaining the base image.

Docker Container

Refers to a runnable instance of a Docker image.

Docker Compose

It enables a developer to define application components i.e. containers, configuration, links, volumes in a single service. A single command is then executed to establish every component in the application and run the application.

Docker Swarm

It's a Docker service in which container nodes function together. It operates as a defined number of instances of a replica task in a Docker image.

Deploying Microservices with Kubernetes

Kubernetes is a recent technology in deploying microservices. It extends Docker capabilities, since Linux containers can be managed in a single system. It also allows the management and running of Docker containers across multiple hosts offering co-location of containers, service discovery, and replication control. Kubernetes has become an extremely powerful approach in deploying microservices, especially for large-scale microservices deployments.

Summary

We have discussed that for microservices to be deployed effectively, developers should adhere to the best deployment practices, as discussed in this chapter. Containers are effective in microservices deployment as they isolate services. Microservices can be deployed using either Docker or Kubernetes, as discussed above,

Chapter 7 – Security in Microservices

Securing microservices is a requirement for an enterprise running their applications or websites on microservices, since data breaches or hacking are very common these days and can lead to massive unwarranted loses. As much as security in an organization is everyone's responsibility, microservices should be secured after their deployment, as we are going to discuss in this chapter. First, let's look at security in monolithic applications.

Security in Monolithic Applications

As we discussed earlier, monolithic applications are deployed dependently, thereby they have a large surface area in an application compared to microservices. The fact that microservices are isolated from each other and deployed independently means that they are more secure, compared to monoliths. However, implementing security in microservices can be challenging. The monolithic application has different attack vectors from microservices, and their security is implemented as follows.

- Security in a typical monolithic application is about finding 'who is the intruder' and 'what can they do' and how do we propagate the information.

- After establishing this information, security is then implemented from a common security component which is at the beginning of the request handling chain. The component uses an underlying user respiratory or a store to populate the required information.

This is done through an authentication (auth) mechanism, which verifies the identity of a user and manages what they can or cannot access through permissions. Data from client to the server is then secured through encryption achieved through HTTPS protocol. In a.Net monolithic application, a user files a request to a web application through a web browser which requires them to enter their username and password. This request is then transferred through HTTPS and load balancer to the Auth, which then connects to the user credential store container, such as SQL server, which contains login details of various users. The user-supplied credentials i.e. username and password, are then verified against the ones retrieved from credentials store by the auth layer.

On verification, the user's browser automatically creates a cookie session, enabling him or her to access the requested information. In this kind of monolithic application, security is achieved by ensuring that the application modules do not separate verification and validation of request while communicating with each other.

Security in Microservices

Security in microservices architecture is achieved by translating the pattern used in securing monolithic applications to microservices. In microservices, the authentication layer is broken into microservices in different applications, which will need its authentication mechanisms. The user credential store is different for every microservices. From our previous discussion, this pattern cannot be implemented, since auth cannot be synced across all devices, and validating inter-process communication might be impossible. Additionally, modern applications based on Android or iOS cannot support secure information between clients and services, since session-based authentication using cookies is not possible, as in monolithic applications.So, the question is how these problems are solved to secure microservices application. The solution comes in the form of OpenID Connect, JSON Web Tokens and OAuth 2.0, as we will discuss below.

JSON Web Tokens

JSON Web Tokens(JWT) is used in producing a data structure which contains information about the issuer and the recipient, along with the sender's identity. They can be deployed independently, irrespective of OAuth 2.0 or OPENID Connect, as they are not tied together. The tokens are secured with symmetric and asymmetric keys to ensure information received by a client is authentic or trustable.

The OAuth 2.0

The OAuth 2.0 is an authorization framework that lets a third-party application to obtain finite access to a HTTP service, either on behalf of the resource owner by orchestrating an approval interaction between the resource owner and the HTTP service, or by allowing the third-party application to obtain access on its behalf. OAuth 2.0 functions as a

215

delegated authorization framework, relying on authentication mechanisms to complete authorization framework. The figure below illustrates the functionality of OAuth in securing microservices.

OpenID Connect

It comes top of OAuth 2.0 protocol and its importance in the user authentication i.e. standard for authentication. It allows a client to verify end users based on the authentication performed by an authorization server. It is also used to obtainthe basic profile information of end users. Clients using any device, i.e. web-based, mobile and javascript can access information relating to authenticated sessions and end users through OpenID Connect. Validation of the end user is through sending ID token to an application used by a client.

To understand microservices security, let's use an example of a client requesting a service through his/ her mobile-based microservices application.

OAuth and the OpenID Connect (Authorization Server)authenticates the client to access data in the microservices by issuing the Access Token. The API Gateway is the only entry to the application's microservices, then receives the Access Token along with the client's request. The Token Translation at the API Gateway extracts the Access token from the client's request and sends it to the authorization server to retrieve the JSON Web Tokens. JSON tokens, along with the client's request, are then passed to the microservices layer by the API Gateway. JSON Web Token contains the necessary information used in storing user sessions. At each microservices layer, there are components used to process the JSON tokens, thereby obtaining the client's request and its information.

Other Security Practices

There are other practices to secure microservices apart from OAuth 2.0 and Open ID connect, as we are going to discuss below.

Standardization of libraries and frameworks

This refers to introducing libraries and frameworks in the development process. It is done to ease out patching, in case of any vulnerability found. It also minimizes the risk introduced by ad hoc implementation of libraries or tools around development.

Regular vulnerability Identification and mitigation

The vulnerability is regularly checked using an industry-standard vulnerability scanner to scan the source code, coupled with binaries and the findings addressed accordingly.

Third-party audits and penetration testing.

External audits and penetration test are

conducted regularly as they are essential in ensuring data integrity in applications or websites involving sensitive critical data or information

Logging and monitoring

Logging is useful in detecting and recovering from hacking attacks by aggregating logs from different systems and services, thereby essential in microservices security.

Network Segregation

Network segregation or partitioning, although only possible in the monolithicapplication, can be effective in ensuring the security of microservices. This can be achieved through the creation of different network segments and subnets.

Summary

We have discussed that securing microservices is essential to any organization having microservices application systems. Security patterns in a monolithic application cannot be implemented in microservices application due to incompatibility problems, such as each microservices requiring their own authentication mechanism and so on, as discussed in this chapter. Therefore, secure token-based approaches such as OAuth 2.0 and OpenID Connect can be used to secure microservices through authorization and authentication.

Chapter 8 Criticism and Case Study

The emergence of microservices as a technique in software application development has been largely criticized for some reasons, namely:

- Information barriers due to services

- Communication of services over a network is costly in terms of network latency and message processing time

- Complexity in testing and deployment

- Difficulty in moving responsibilities between services. It involves communication between different teams, rewriting the functionality in another language or fitting it into a different infrastructure.

- Too many services, if not deployed

correctly, may slow system performance.

- Additional complexity, such as network latency, message formats, load balancing and fault tolerance.

Nano service

Nano service refers to anti-patterns where a service is too fine-grained, meaning that the overheads outweighs its utility. Microservices have continually been criticized as a Nano service due to numerous problems such as the code overhead, runtime overhead, and fragmented logic. However, there are some proposed alternatives to the Nano service. These are:

- Packaging the functionality as software library rather than a service.

- Combining the functionality with other functionalities to produce a more substantial useful service

- Refactoring the system by putting

the functionality in other services or redesigning the system altogether.

Design for Failure

Microservices have been criticized as prone to failure compared to monoliths, since they introduce isolated services to the system, which increases the possibility of having a system failure. Some of the reasons that may lead to failure in microservices include network instability and unavailability of the underlying resources. However, there are certain design mechanisms that may ensure an unavailable or unresponsive microservices does not cause the whole application to fail. It ensures that microservices is fault tolerant and swiftly recovers after experiencing a failure. In microservices, it is important to maintain real-time monitoring, since services can fail at any time. The failures should be repaired quickly to be able to restore the services. Let's discuss common ways of avoiding failure in

223

microservices application.

Circuit Breaker

A circuit breaker is a fault monitor component which is configured to each service in the application. The fault monitor then observes service failures, and when they reach a certain threshold, the circuit breaker stops any further requests to the services. This is essential in avoiding unnecessary resource consumption by requesting delay timeouts. It is also important in monitoring the whole system.

Bulkhead

Since microservices applications comprise of numerous services, a failure in one service may affect the functioning of other microservices, or even the entire application. Bulkhead is essential in preventing a failure in one microservices from affecting the whole application, as it isolates different parts of the microservices application

Timeout

Timeout is a pattern mechanism to prevent clients from overwaiting for a response from microservices once they have sent as a request through there devices. Clients configure a time interval in which they are comfortable to wait for increasing efficiency and client satisfaction.

These patterns are configured to the API Gateway, and monitors the response of the microservices once they receive a request. When a service is unresponsive or unavailable, the Timeout mechanism notifies the user to try accessing the microservices another time to avoid overloading the application system and prevent failure in one service from affecting the other microservices. Additionally, the Gateway can be used as the central point to monitor each microservices, thereby informing developers of a failure.

Microservices Disrupting the Fintech Industries

Microservices have greatly disrupted the Fintech industries and other sectors. By breaking down big, complex systems into smaller pieces or services, microservices allow complicated work to be divided and distributed amongst smaller teams, making it easier to develop, test, and deploy. Fintech industries are realizing that they are being disrupted and need to reinvent them to compete against these digital-only businesses. The speed of innovation is dictated by the ability to expose business assets in a digital-friendly manner, and in some instances leverage external assets to provide a more social experience. The core paradigm enabling the use of business assets within mobile or tablet applications is through microservices. For a large majority of enterprises, microservices have become a new business channel to expose key assets, data, or services for consumption by mobile, web, internet of things, and enterprise applications. It can represent monetary benefit by metering usage of API services, and providing different plans (i.e. Gold, Silver Bronze) at various price-points, or simply making them available at no-charge to increase usage and brand promotion through increased marketing.

Companies using Microservices

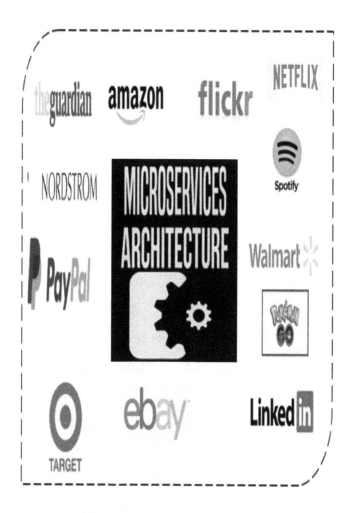

Chapter 9 –Summary

We have discussed a lot about microservices from their invention, definition, advantages, building, integration techniques, deployment, and finally their security. In this chapter, we are going to recap what we have already discussed.

Before Microservices?

As we had discussed, before the invention of microservices, monolithic architecture and Service-Oriented Architecture was used to develop software applications

Monolithic Architecture

Monolithic architecture consists of components such as user interface, business logic, and database access, which are interconnected and interdependent. Therefore, a minor change inany module of the application results in a change to the entire application. This would require the redeployment of the entire application. Monolithic architecture has numerous challenges, including code complexity, scalability, large interdependent code, and difficulty in the adoption of a new technology in terms of application or new devices.

Service-oriented architecture

Service-oriented architecture is an improvement of monolithic architecture resolving some of the challenges we mentioned above. Services primarily started with SOA and it's the main concept behind it. As we have already defined, a service is a piece of program or code providing some functionality to the system components. SOA comes with some advantages, such as the ability to reuse codes, and the ability to upgrade applications without necessarily deploying the entire application.

Microservices architecture.

Microservices architecture is very

similar to SOA, except that services are deployed independently. A change in a piece of program or code does not change the functionality of the entire application. For services to function independently, a certain discipline and strategy are required. Some of the disadvantages we discussed include clear boundaries, easy deployment, technology adaptation, affordable scalability, and quick market response.

Building Microservices from Monoliths

We discussed building microservices from an existing monolithic application. First is to identify decomposition candidates within a monolith based on parameters including code complexity, technology adaptation, resource requirement, and human dependency. Second is the identification of seams, which act as boundaries in microservices, then the separation can start. Seams should be picked on the right parameters depending on module interdependency, team structure, database. and existing technology. The master database should be handled with care through a separate service or configuration. An advantage of microservices having its own database is that it removes many of the existing foreign key relationships, thereby has a high transaction-handling ability.

Integration Techniques

Microservices integration techniques are mainly based on communication between microservices. We discussed that there are two ways in which microservices communicate: synchronous and asynchronous communication. Synchronous communication is based on request/response, while asynchronous style is event-based. Integration patterns are essential to facilitate complex interaction among microservices. We discussed integrating microservices using event-driven patterns in the API Gateway. The event-driven pattern works by some services publishing their events, and some subscribing to those available events. The subscribing services simply react independently to the event-publishing services, based on the event and its metadata.

Deployment.

We discussed microservices deployment and how it can be challenging for various reasons. Breaking the central database further increases the overall challenges. Microservices deployment requires continuous delivery(CD) and continuous integration (CI) right from the initial stages. Infrastructure can be represented with codes for easy deployment using tools such as CFEngine, Chef, Puppet, and PowerShell DSC. Microservices can be deployed using Docker or Kubernetes after containerization.

Testing microservices

We discussed the test pyramid

representing the types of test. Unit test is used to verify small functionalities in the entire application, while system test is used to verify the entire application on its functionality. The mock and stub approach is used in microservices testing. This approach makes testing independent of other microservices and eliminates challenges in testing the application's database due to mock database interactions. Integration testing is concerned with external microservices communicating with them in the process. This is done through mocking external services.

Security

Securing microservices is essential to an organization to ensure data integrity. In a monolithic application, security is attained through having a single point of authentication and authorization. However, this approach is not possible in microservices architecture, since each service needs to be secured independently. Therefore, the OAuth 2.0

authorization framework, coupled with OpenID Connect, is used to secure microservices. OAuth 2.0's main role is to authorize clients into the application system as we discussed in *chapter 7*. One provider of OAuth 2.0 and OpenID Connect is the Azure Active Directory (Azure AD)

Conclusive Remarks

It is our hope that this book has been essential in your understanding of the microservices architecture by answering all your questions based on this wide subject. Microservices architecture is a pretty new concept, and is still in development. Therefore, the contents of this book may change overtime.

My Other Books available across the platforms in e-book, paperback and audible versions:

1. **Blockchain Technology : Introduction to Blockchain Technology and its impact on Business Ecosystem**

2. DevOps Handbook: Introduction to DevOps and its Impact on Business Ecosystem

3. Blockchain Technology and DevOps : Introduction and Impact on Business Ecosystem

4. **Love Yourself: 21 day plan for learning "Self-Love" to cultivate self-worth ,self-belief, self-confidence & happiness**

5. Intermittent Fasting: 7 effective techniques of Intermittent Fasting

7 EFFECTIVE TECHNIQUES OF

INTERMITTENT FASTING

Stay Healthy,Lose Weight,
Slow Down Aging Process & Live Longer!

STEPHEN FLEMING

6. Love Yourself and intermittent Fasting(Mind and Body Bundle Book)

You can check all my Books on my **Amazon's Author Page**

** If you prefer audible versions of these books, I have few free coupons, mail me at valueadd2life@gmail.com. If available, I would mail you the same.

www.ingramcontent.com/pod-product-compliance
Lightning Source LLC
Chambersburg PA
CBHW071240050326
40690CB00011B/2194